DATE DUE

Black
Abolitionists

Other books in the
Profiles in History series:

❧   ❧   ❧

Black Women Activists
Leaders of the Civil Rights Movement
Terrorist Leaders

❧

Black Abolitionists

Profiles · in · History

Karin Coddon, *Book Editor*

Bruce Glassman, *Vice President*
Bonnie Szumski, *Publisher*
Helen Cothran, *Managing Editor*

GREENHAVEN
PRESS ®

THOMSON
───── ✳ ─────
GALE

San Diego • Detroit • New York • San Francisco • Cleveland
New Haven, Conn. • Waterville, Maine • London • Munich

For more information, contact
Greenhaven Press
27500 Drake Rd.
Farmington Hills, MI 48331-3535
Or you can visit our Internet site at http://www.gale.com

Cover credit: © CORBIS
Dover, 21
National Archives, 91

LIBRARY OF CONGRESS CATALOGING-IN-PUBLICATION DATA

Black abolitionists / Karin Coddon, book editor.
    p. cm. — (Profiles in history)
  Includes bibliographical references and index.
  ISBN 0-7377-1711-4 (alk. paper)
    1. African American abolitionists—History. 2. African American abolitionists—History—Sources. 3. African American abolitionists—Biography. 4. Antislavery movements—United States—History. 5. Antislavery movements—United States—History—Sources. I. Coddon, Karin. II. Series.
  E441.B57 2004
  973.7'114'092396073—dc21   2003049015

Printed in the United States of America

Contents

Chapter 1: The Origins of Black Abolitionism

proposal to resettle blacks in Africa that was advocated by many white opponents of slavery.

Chapter 2: Frederick Douglass: The Voice of Freedom

Chapter 3: Harriet Tubman: Heroine of the Underground Railroad

Chapter 4: Other Groundbreakers

Foreword

Historians and other scholars have often argued about which forces are most influential in driving the engines of history. A favorite theory in past ages was that powerful supernatural forces—the gods and/or fate—were deciding factors in earthly events. Modern theories, by contrast, have tended to emphasize more natural and less mysterious factors. In the nineteenth century, for example, the great Scottish historian Thomas Carlyle stated, "No great man lives in vain. The history of the world is but the biography of great men." This was the kernel of what came to be known as the "great man" theory of history, the idea that from time to time an unusually gifted, influential man or woman emerges and pushes the course of civilization in a new direction. According to Carlyle:

> Universal History, the history of what man has accomplished in this world, is at bottom the History of the Great Men who have worked here. They were the leaders of men, these great ones; the modelers . . . of whatsoever the general mass of men contrived to do or to attain; all things that we see standing accomplished in the world are properly the outer material result. . . . The soul of the whole world's history, it may justly be considered, were the history of these [persons].

In this view, individuals such as Moses, Buddha, Augustus, Christ, Constantine, Elizabeth I, Thomas Jefferson, Frederick Douglass, Franklin Roosevelt, and Nelson

Mandela accomplished deeds or promoted ideas that sooner or later reshaped human societies in large portions of the globe.

The great man thesis, which was widely popular in the late 1800s and early 1900s, has since been eclipsed by other theories of history. Some scholars accept the "situational" theory. It holds that human leaders and innovators only react to social situations and movements that develop substantially on their own, through random interactions. In this view, Moses achieved fame less because of his unique personal qualities and more because he wisely dealt with the already existing situation of the Hebrews wandering in the desert in search of a new home.

More widely held, however, is a view that in a sense combines the great man and situational theories. Here, major historical periods and political, social, and cultural movements occur when a group of gifted, influential, and like-minded individuals respond to a situation or need over the course of time. In this scenario, Moses is seen as one of a group of prophets who over the course of centuries established important traditions of monotheism; and over time a handful of ambitious, talented pharaohs led ancient Egypt from its emergence as the world's first nation to its great age of conquest and empire. Likewise, the Greek playwrights Sophocles and Euripides, the Elizabethan playwright Shakespeare, and the American playwright Eugene O'Neill all advanced the art of drama, leading it to its present form.

The books in the Profiles in History series chronicle and examine in detail the leading figures in some of history's most important historical periods and movements. Some, like those covering Egypt's leading pharaohs and the most influential U.S. presidents, deal with national leaders guiding a great people through good times and bad. Other volumes in the series examine the leaders of important, constructive social movements, such as those that sought to abolish slavery in the nineteenth century and fought for human rights in the twentieth century. And some, such as the one on Hitler and his henchmen, profile far less constructive, though no less historically important, groups of leaders.

Each book in the series begins with a detailed essay providing crucial background information on the historical period or movement being covered. The main body of the volume consists of a series of shorter essays, each covering an important individual in that period or movement. Where appropriate, two or more essays are devoted to a particularly influential person. Some of the essays provide biographical information; while others, including primary sources by or about the person, focus in on his or her specific deeds, ideas, speeches, or followers. More primary source documents, providing further detail, appear in an appendix, followed by a chronology of events and a thorough, up-to-date bibliography that guides interested readers to further research. Overall, the volumes of the Profiles in History series offer a balanced view of the march of civilization by demonstrating how certain individuals make history and at the same time are products of the deeds and movements of their predecessors.

Introduction

The abolitionist movement was one of the most important and radical reform movements of the nineteenth century. Often ridiculed, demonized, repressed, and targeted for violence by proslavery factions, the abolitionists fearlessly maintained their antislavery activism, which included public lectures; publication and circulation of fliers, newspapers, and narratives; petitions that largely fell on deaf ears in Washington; and assistance to runaway slaves along the Underground Railroad. Over one hundred years before the civil rights movement forced the nation to address racial segregation, African American men and women courageously flouted social strictures and risked their lives and liberty in order to take active roles in the struggle for emancipation. Far from passive victims of an oppressive system and a largely indifferent white majority, black abolitionists demanded that the universal equality invoked in the Declaration of Independence be applied to all, regardless of color.

Racial Difference and the Antislavery Movement

Abolitionism was, however, neither a grassroots movement nor a monolithic one characterized by a single set of beliefs. Even as the divided nation teetered on the brink of war in 1860, a majority of Northerners did not consider themselves abolitionists, a fact that Abraham

Lincoln took into consideration when he initially argued that the war's aim was to preserve the Union, not to abolish slavery. Some Northerners even sympathized with Southern complaints about abolitionist "agitation"—the alleged incursion of antislavery literature and activists into its region with the express purpose of encouraging insurrection and escape among bondsmen and bondswomen. Many white Northerners feared that abolition would prompt an influx of black people from the South to compete with free labor for jobs and unsettle the strict racial segregation that characterized the nation as a whole from colonial days until the latter half of the twentieth century.

If abolitionism was, then, not a "popular" movement, neither was it a wholly uniform one. Abolitionists differed among themselves over the role of women, the relevance of direct political engagement, the uses of violent resistance, and the question of racial and social equality. The movement was fraught with factionalism: publisher William Lloyd Garrison urged his followers to reject political activities and focus on moral persuasion, while leading black abolitionist, writer, and lecturer Frederick Douglass cautiously advocated that abolitionists petition the existing political system as a means toward universal liberty. Douglass in turn broke with black radicals such as Henry Highland Garnet, who endorsed slave rebellion and violence as legitimate modes of resistance. For many white progressives, abolitionism was part of a larger nineteenth-century reform movement that also endorsed woman suffrage, universal education, and temperance; for blacks, however, abolitionism was both paramount and personal, a matter of basic human rights and the survival of a people.

Because black abolitionists believed emancipation was more than a noble yet impersonal abstraction, they were able to contribute in a uniquely powerful, authoritative way to the antislavery movement. Many leading black abolitionists—Douglass, Garnet, William Wells Brown, Harriet Jacobs, Harriet Tubman—were themselves fugitive slaves who spoke and wrote of their firsthand experiences, which included physical abuse, destruction of family, and harrowing escapes. They provided human faces and voices to testify to the iniquities of the slave system, a fact not lost on the many Northerners who had little direct knowledge of slavery. The learnedness and eloquence of black abolitionists such as Douglass, Brown, John Mercer Langston, and Maria Stewart refuted the common assumption—even among some whites opposed to slavery—that African Americans were intellectually inferior. The courage of Harriet Tubman, for example, who risked her life and freedom countless times to lead runaway slaves to liberty along the Underground Railroad, stirred some Northern sympathies as potently as abolitionist speeches and literature.

Early African American Abolition

Colonial America was as sectionally divided over slavery as the new nation would be during the Civil War. The agricultural southern colonies were almost from inception sustained by slave labor even as the North continued to urbanize and industrialize, which contributed to its willingness to prohibit slavery entirely by the beginning of the nineteenth century. Although the constitutional framers deliberately sidestepped the issue of slavery lest the southern states refuse ratification, African Americans had already played a vital part in the original struggle for independence. Crispus Attucks was among the resisters killed in the Boston Massacre, and black volunteers such as Peter Salem (a hero at the Battle of Bunker Hill) and James Forten served in the revolutionary army.

In the early nineteenth century, two key phenomena

helped lay the groundwork for the emergence of an organized black abolitionist movement in the 1830s. One was the formation of the first official, all-black Christian church in America in 1816: the African Methodist Episcopal Church, founded in Boston by ministers Richard Allen and Absalom Jones. The church became the heart of the black community in the Northeast, where most free blacks lived in the antebellum United States. While some black ministers admonished their flock to accept racial injustice with Christian resignation and await divine vindication in the afterlife, many more spoke from the pulpit of the evils of slavery and exhorted all good Christians to oppose the institution. The early black churches also provided meeting places where African Americans could discuss political issues and organize antislavery activities.

The second foundational early trend that influenced later abolitionists was the issue of black repatriation to Africa, organized by the American Colonization Society (ACS). Historian C. Peter Ripley has characterized the procolonizationists as

> a mix of diverse interests that came together to settle free blacks and newly emancipated slaves in Africa. Most colonizationists believed that free blacks endangered American society. They accepted the popular myth that blacks lacked the moral character and ability to become useful citizens. Even whites who considered slavery evil reasoned that sending blacks to a colony in Africa would ease white anxieties and thereby encourage manumissions, and at the same time provide free blacks with a refuge from American oppression. Most white abolitionists and antislavery organizations at the time supported colonization.[1]

By the time the colonization movement emerged, well over one hundred thousand free blacks lived in the Northeast, and the vast majority responded angrily to

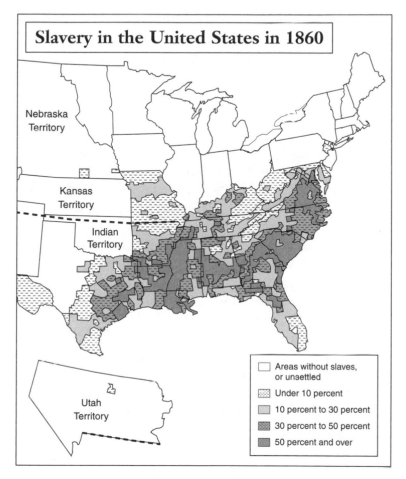

Slavery in the United States in 1860

Nebraska Territory

Kansas Territory

Indian Territory

Utah Territory

☐ Areas without slaves, or unsettled

▨ Under 10 percent

▨ 10 percent to 30 percent

▨ 30 percent to 50 percent

■ 50 percent and over

the proposal that they uproot their lives and relinquish their American identity. As Ripley points out, the northern black community's resistance to colonization was a turning point in the fledgling abolitionist movement: "Free blacks . . . rejected colonization as a threat to their future on the American continent."[2] David Walker, a fiery black radical, helped found the Massachusetts General Colored Association in 1826 largely in opposition to colonizationism, and he published his famous treatise on black nationalism, the *Appeal . . . to the Coloured Citizens of the World*, three years later.

Black leaders attempted to dissuade prominent whites sympathetic to colonization and embrace emancipation. Eventually, some began to relinquish the idea of colonization. Abolitionist William Lloyd Garrison inaugurated a new, radicalized era for the antislavery movement. Fewer white abolitionists espoused gradual and voluntary emancipation, and, in turn, black activists became increasingly influenced by the great nineteenth-century reform movement that would spawn social campaigns for women's rights, temperance, and education and prison reforms as well as for emancipation. The American Anti-Slavery Society was established in late 1833 as a coalition of black and white abolitionists.

Before westward expansion forced Congress to reopen the debate over slavery that most politicians—northern as well as southern—had contentedly preferred to ignore, the burgeoning abolitionist movement provided the only major forum for public dissent over the institution's morality and legality. Northerners tended to view abolitionists as fanatics and troublemakers who were not representative of the region's overall attitudes, and southerners raged against the perceived interference in a regional institution most of them cherished as fundamental to their way of life. Many northerners also were affronted by the intermingling of blacks and whites, women and men, that was becoming increasingly common within the abolitionist movement (although a number of white male abolitionists also disapproved of the practice). As for southerners, they blamed the violent uprising instigated by Nat Turner in 1831 on the evils of abolitionism, but more often, abolitionists were the victims of mob violence, and usually on their home turf in the North. Several thousand demonstrators amassed outside a Boston women's antislavery meeting in 1835, disrupting the assembly and threatening the lives of William Lloyd Garrison and George

Thompson, the English abolitionist who had been invited to address the group. In 1837 abolitionist publisher Elijah Lovejoy was murdered in Alton, Illinois, by a bloodthirsty throng that included several of the town's most reputable citizens. In 1838 a mob descended on Pennsylvania Hall in Philadelphia, where another women's antislavery convention was gathering, and burned the structure to the ground before setting off to attack the home of Quaker abolitionist Lucretia Mott, who had fortunately taken refuge elsewhere.

But while black and white abolitionists refused to be intimidated into curtailing their antislavery activities and often worked in concert to help fugitives elude would-be captors, their relationship was still marked by a degree of tension. As professor Charles Johnson and journalist Patricia Smith point out, some white abolitionists reacted to their black counterparts with either unease or condescension:

> The difference between black and white abolitionists was most apparent when the two groups worked closely together. The whites, mindful of their destiny to deliver the underclass, patronized their black coworkers. And the blacks' refusal to fit the image of the humble subservient unnerved many of their white colleagues.[3]

But by the 1840s black abolitionists gained an authority that their white counterparts could not: the authority of firsthand experience recounted in what was coming to be a widely popular new genre of literature, the slave narrative.

The Power of the Written Word

The abolitionist movement was notable for the participation of some of the most powerful orators of the age: Frederick Douglass, William Wells Brown, Sojourner Truth, Henry Highland Garnet. But the movement was equally galvanized by the power—and reach—of the written word. President Abraham Lincoln was reported to have teased Harriet Beecher Stowe, author of *Uncle Tom's Cabin* (1852), that she was the "little woman who wrote the book that made this great war," with her novel's wrenching, if sentimental, portrait of slavery. However, the personal narratives of former slaves found a wide readership from the 1840s onward, certainly laying the literary groundwork for Stowe's best seller and, even more importantly, offering to their audiences a firsthand account of the cruelties of the slave system told by those lucky enough to escape to freedom. The memoirs attested to physical and mental abuses, including torture, rape, and the destruction of families. Northern readers of slave narratives, many of whom had never directly witnessed the slave system, included countless middle-class women influenced by Victorian-era idealism concerning motherhood and the sanctity of the family; they were especially affected by the harrowing accounts of children wrenched from mothers' arms to be sold to distant owners and never seen again by their kin. Because slave narratives were published with a middle-class white audience in mind, they often had what Richard Newman, Patrick Rael, and Philip Lapsansky have termed a "somewhat formulaic quality":

> Black autobiographies were sometimes shaped by white editors and copyists, who might, for example, overemphasize religiosity as a means of black redemption or the kindness of white abolitionists. Slave narrator Henry Bibb's editors excised many angry references to whites and highlighted the aid of white reformers on the Underground Railroad. Bibb's second edition, published by himself, told a somewhat different story, with Bibb emphasizing his own agency in fleeing slavery and a none-too-subtle anger at apathetic whites.[4]

But regardless of the occasional mollification of the

indignities and horrors of bondage, the memoirs were far more than quasi-journalistic accounts of life under slavery. They were also, and perhaps even more significantly, articulations of the humanity and dignity of black people, powerfully challenging the proslavery argument that those of African descent were subhuman and thus innately fit only for servitude, a position also shared by many in the racist North. African American studies scholar Henry Louis Gates underscores the importance of the slave narratives not only as unique documents of suffering but also as literary testimonials to the bondsperson's desire for freedom:

Abraham Lincoln

> One of the most curious aspects of the African person's enslavement in the New World is that he and she *wrote* about the severe conditions of their bondage within what with understatement came to be called "the peculiar institution." In the long history of human bondage, it was only the black slaves in the United States who—once secure and free in the North, and with the generous encouragement and assistance of northern abolitionists—created a *genre* of literature that at once testified against their captors and bore witness to the urge of every black slave to be free and literate. Hundreds of ex-slaves felt compelled to tell their tales on the anti-slavery lecture circuit in the North and in the written form of the autobiographical narrative. As several scholars have shown, there is an inextricable link in the Afro-American tradition between literacy and freedom.[5]

Long before the Emancipation Proclamation and the

Thirteenth Amendment, slave narratives were compellingly making the case for common humanity and equal rights. Gates estimates that by the end of the Civil War over one hundred book-length slave memoirs had been published, with thousands of captivity narratives appearing in shorter forms.

The Underground Railroad

A central narrative feature of most slave memoirs was the escape, usually an event described with utmost dramatic tension and suspense. But most authors took particular care not to reveal the specifics of their respective flights from bondage. In fact, so much necessary secrecy shrouded the operations of the Underground Railroad, as the loosely structured network of escape routes and safe houses came to be known, that it remains to this day difficult to ascertain how many runaways reached their goal of freedom in the Northeast or Canada, what exact paths they took, and the identities of all those who helped them. Until the latter part of the twentieth century, historians tended to emphasize the role of white abolitionists, especially Quakers, in assisting fugitives along their way to freedom; Harriet Tubman, the most famous "conductor," was typically presented as a kind of noble black exception. Certainly many eminent white abolitionists—including Henry David Thoreau, Levi Coffin, and Thomas Garrett—played integral and courageous roles in the railroad's operations, even after the enactment of the Fugitive Slave Law of 1850 criminalized the assistance of runaway slaves along with the act of escape itself. But subsequent historiography has recognized that black abolitionists were equally vital to the Underground Railroad and risked even more since many of them were also, according to the law, fugitive slaves. Frederick Douglass, William Wells Brown, William Still, and

Robert Purvis were among the numerous black activists who participated in the railroad's covert operations. If the 1850 Fugitive Slave Law served to render escape from slavery both riskier and more imperative, the landmark *Dred Scott* decision seven years later signaled to most abolitionists that the prospects for emancipation were growing dimmer, not more hopeful, despite the dogged efforts of the antislavery movement. In his ruling, Supreme Court justice Roger B. Taney wrote that Dred Scott, a former slave who had rightfully claimed his liberty upon moving to the free state of Illinois, could in fact be lawfully reenslaved upon his return to Missouri. Taney explicitly denied blacks the fundamental status of citizenship. Proslavery forces, already mobilized by their fight to ensure that slavery be permitted in the western territories acquired in the aftermath of the Mexican War, hoped fervently that the *Dred Scott* decision would prove a death knell for the abolitionist movement. Yet Frederick Douglass spoke for many in his response to *Dred Scott:*

> We are now told . . . that the day is lost—all lost— and that we might as well give up the struggle. The highest authority has spoken. The voice of the Supreme Court has gone out over the troubled waves of the National Conscience . . . [But] my hopes were never brighter than now.
>
> I have no fear that the National Conscience will be put to sleep by such an open, glaring, and scandalous tissue of lies.[6]

Indeed, *Dred Scott* was greeted with outrage and dismay not only by abolitionists but also by members of the fledgling Republican Party (founded in 1854 as a loose coalition of disenchanted Whigs, "free-soilers" opposed to slavery's expansion, and antislavery activists). Even Stephen Douglas, the U.S. senator from Illinois and an outspoken racist, decried *Dred Scott* as a federal usurpation of the "states' rights" that he so ardently advocated. By the end of the 1850s it was becoming obvious to all parties engaged in the slavery controversy that the nation was careening toward a monumental crisis, what William Seward, the antislavery Republican senator from New York, termed an *irrepressible conflict*. White radical abolitionist John Brown and a small band of followers seized control of the federal arsenal at Harpers Ferry, Virginia, in October 1859, a move designed to incite slaves to armed rebellion. Brown and his men were overcome by federal troops, most of his followers were killed, and the leader himself was arrested, swiftly tried, and executed. But the incident became the penultimate watershed moment for both proslavery and antislavery movements. Although some abolitionists, including Frederick Douglass, had been leery of Brown's militancy, many others, such as Tubman (who had met with Brown and assisted his recruitment of the Harpers Ferry raiders), Thoreau, and Garrison, viewed Brown as a hero and a martyr. For Southerners, John Brown embodied their worst suspicions about the abolitionist movement, whose violent fanaticism would stop at nothing, they believed, until all slaves were forcibly freed, the white race's supremacy toppled, and the Southern "way of life" (a common euphemism for the slave system) destroyed.

Lincoln's Election, the Secession Crisis, and Civil War

The incident at Harpers Ferry culminated a decade of increasing tensions. Less than a year later, Southern states reacted to the election of Republican Abraham Lincoln as though John Brown himself had been raised from the dead to lead the country. Southerners viewed Lincoln's election as a virtual declaration of war. Barely a month after the November 1860 election, South Carolina became the first Southern state to secede from the Union. For their part, abolitionists viewed Lincoln's election with mixed feelings and even suspicion. Although throughout his presidential campaign he had been forthright in voicing his moral opposition to slavery, Lincoln believed that the federal government had no power to abolish the institution by fiat. Before the outbreak of the Civil War, Lincoln often expressed hope that slavery would end through voluntary and gradual emancipation, with the former owners compensated monetarily for their economic losses; he also briefly entertained the viability of colonization. Keenly aware that most Northerners would not support a war waged in the name of emancipation, Lincoln insisted throughout the first year and a half of his presidency that the conflict that had riven the nation was over the Union, not slavery, an assertion that rankled abolitionists.

Lincoln was also concerned about the border states—Maryland, Delaware, Kentucky, and Missouri—that remained in the Union, hence, the Emancipation Proclamation, announced September 1862 and becoming law January 1, 1863, pointedly freed slaves only in Confederate states. Black abolitionists, particularly Frederick Douglass, played an important role in pressuring Lincoln to act decisively on the slavery issue. While some radical abolitionists were disappointed with the limitations of the Emancipation Proclamation, most—including Douglass and William Lloyd Garrison—were unequivocal in their celebration. "We shout with joy," wrote Douglass, "that we live to record this righteous decree."

Douglass's relationship with Lincoln during the war in many ways embodied both the remarkable gains black abolitionists had made in having a voice in the political sphere and the constraints they continued to face from a fundamentally racist North and a president who was seen by many activists (as well as by radical Republicans in his own party) as at times maddeningly cautious and lawyerly. Almost from the outbreak of the Civil War Douglass was lobbying not only for emancipation but also for the right of black soldiers to serve in the Union army, as many were eager to do. Although Lincoln ultimately came around to Douglass's way of thinking on both matters, his conciliatory stance toward the seceded South prompted Douglass, along with several other prominent abolitionists, to support former Union army general John C. Fremont in his 1864 bid for the presidency. Fremont's 1861 effort to free slaves in Missouri had been overruled by Lincoln, an incident that won the former man abolitionist plaudits while seeming to confirm the antislavery movement's wariness toward the latter. Nonetheless, most abolitionists came around to supporting Lincoln's reelection. Frederick Douglass even attended the second inaugural festivities in the nation's capital. When police tried to refuse Douglass entry into the White House, Lincoln himself intervened, ushering him into the reception, as described by Stephen B. Oates:

> "Here comes my friend Douglass," the President announced when Douglass entered the room. "I am glad to see you," Lincoln told him. "I saw you in the crowd today, listening to my address." He added, "There is no man in the country whose opinion I value more than yours. I want to know what you think of it." Douglass said he was impressed; he thought it "a sacred effort." "I am glad you liked it!" Lincoln said as Douglass passed down the line. It was the first inaugural reception in the history of the Republic in which an American President had greeted a free black man and solicited his opinion.[7]

Douglass's prominence as a leader had certainly caught the president's attention and earned his respect. But

Douglass's activism during the war was not unique. Other well-known black abolitionists (including Langston, Garnet, Tubman, and Truth), along with countless ordinary black citizens, committed themselves to the Union war effort, volunteering for military service or recruiting black soldiers, nursing the injured, and helping freed slaves resettle in the North.

Aftermath: The Struggle for Equality Continues

Although many white antislavery activists may have viewed General Robert E. Lee's 1865 surrender at Appomattox as marking the official end of the abolitionist movement, black leaders recognized that the struggle was only beginning. Douglass, Truth, and Langston became outspoken advocates for voting rights and Reconstruction policies that would compensate the former slaves for their sufferings and provide them with the economic assistance without which their emancipation would remain little more than a legal technicality. The assassination of Lincoln less than a week after Lee's surrender inflicted a profound psychic but also political blow to the African American struggle for racial equality. Lincoln's successor, Andrew Johnson, seemed far less interested in solidifying black-white political relations, much to Douglass's consternation. Johnson's concessions to the southern states largely derailed the "radical Reconstruction" espoused by liberal Republicans and former abolitionists; the promised "forty acres and a mule" never materialized, leaving many former slaves to subsist as sharecroppers in conditions sadly comparable to their former state of bondage. "Jim Crow" segregation and Ku Klux Klan terrorism further served to deprive black citizens of the freedoms and rights ostensibly guaranteed them by the Constitution. Postwar black activism itself splintered as so-called accommodationists such as educator Booker T. Washington (1856–1915) exhorted African Americans to pursue practical skills learned under slavery and eschew political agitation, and scholar and intellectual W.E.B. Du Bois (1868–1863) rejected Washington's tacit acceptance of systemic racism and urged fellow blacks to continue to work for radical change. In 1905 the Niagara Movement, spearheaded by Du Bois (who also helped found the National Association for the Advancement of Colored People [NAACP] four years later), formed to advocate a more activist approach to civil rights.

The foundation of the Niagara Movement and the NAACP are often viewed as the beginnings of the modern civil rights movement that came to fruition in the Montgomery, Alabama, bus boycott of the 1950s and the ascendancy of Martin Luther King Jr. as the most influential black American leader of the twentieth century. But in truth, African Americans had been playing key roles as activists and leaders from the nation's very inception. Black abolitionists not only participated in the antislavery movement; they also shaped and empowered it, whether in the rejection of the colonization proposal, the insistence that emancipation be accompanied by all the rights and duties of citizenship (including military service and the franchise), or the recognition that the fight for freedom began rather than ended with the passage of the Thirteenth Amendment, forever prohibiting slavery. Black newspapers, pamphlets, and slave memoirs widely disseminated the argument for freedom, incensing many southerners but also stirring antislavery sympathies throughout the North and Europe. Black speakers—men and women alike—filled public lecture halls, braving the constant threat of mob violence in order to make the case for emancipation. Fugitive slaves risked their own liberty to help other runaways along the Underground Railroad. The legacy of courage and commitment bequeathed by black abolitionists has served to inspire Americans of all races who cherish the principles of justice, equality, and human dignity.

Notes

1. C. Peter Ripley, ed., *Witness for Freedom: African American Voices on Race, Slavery, and Emancipation.* Chapel Hill: University of North Carolina Press, 1993, p. 2.

2. Ripley, *Witness to Freedom*, p. 2.

3. *Africans in America: America's Journey Through Slavery.* San Diego: Harcourt Brace/Harvest, 1998, p. 370.

4. *Pamphlets of Protest: An Anthology of Early African American Protest Literature, 1790–1860.* New York: Routledge, 2001, p. 7.

5. Henry Louis Gates, ed., *The Classic Slave Narratives.* New York: Mentor, 1987, p. ix.

6. Quoted in Charles Johnson, Patricia Smith, and WGBH, eds., *Africans in America: America's Journey Through Slavery.* San Diego: Harcourt Brace/Harvest, 1998, p. 419.

7. *With Malice Toward None: A Life of Abraham Lincoln.* New York: HarperCollins, 1977, p. 412.

CHAPTER

1

Profiles . in . History

The Origins of
Black Abolitionism

James Forten

Ray Allen Billington

James Forten (1766–1842) is among the most accomplished of the early abolitionists. As a young adolescent he served in the U.S. Navy during the Revolutionary War; as an adult he became one of Philadelphia's most affluent businessmen. But despite his achievements and self-made wealth, Forten was outraged by the racism and discrimination to which all black Americans, even those freeborn as he was, were subjected on a daily basis. He turned his passions to the emerging abolitionist movement, especially in his home state of Pennsylvania, tirelessly lobbying, writing pamphlets, and contributing generously from his personal fortune to the cause of freedom and equality. The following biographical profile by Ray Allen Billington details Forten's progress from Revolutionary War naval powder boy to eminent businessman and civic leader, and from there to dedicated antislavery and civil rights crusader whose efforts further radicalized the white abolitionist movement led by William Lloyd Garrison.

Ray Allen Billington was among the most eminent scholars of American history. He taught at several U.S. universities as well as at England's Oxford University. His book *Land of Savagery; Land of Promise: The European Image of the American Frontier in the Nineteenth Century* (1981) is considered a landmark study of the American frontier experience.

Ray Allen Billington, "Introduction," *The Journal of Charlotte L. Forten: A Free Negro in the Slave Era*, edited by Ray Allen Billington. New York: Crollier Books, 1961.

❧ ❧ ❧

James Forten's attention was directed toward the plight of the slaves virtually from the day of his birth. Born in 1766 of free Negro parents, he received a fragmentary education in the school of Anthony Benezet, famed Quaker abolitionist, before volunteering as powder boy aboard a Philadelphia privateer during the Revolution. No sooner was the war over than he displayed the rebellious spirit that marked his later career. Why, he asked himself, should he stay in a land that proclaimed all men equal yet condemned those of darker skins to second-class citizenship? Why not escape to England, where men were judged by character rather than by color? These were the motives that drove him abroad for an important twelve-month period. In Britain he met more abolitionists—earnest young men, such as Granville Sharpe, who were lifting their voices against the slave trade and forced labor in the colonies. Young Forten listened entranced to their pleas; here indeed was a cause worth fighting—and dying—for. During that year he became an avowed abolitionist, ready to dedicate his life to the crusade against slavery.

Back in his native land, Forten soon established himself as a leader of the Philadelphia Negro community. Apprenticed to a sailmaker, he displayed such skill that he was made foreman when only twenty and became proprietor of the establishment twelve years later. According to contemporary records, his invention of a device to handle sails earned him a fortune of $100,000. While amassing this sum he found time for innumerable civil activities, ranging from helping to defend Philadelphia during the War of 1812 to serving as a pioneer member of one of the city's first Negro churches.

A wealthy and respected citizen, he might well have settled into a life of affluent indolence, with never a thought for the less fortunate members of his race.

Forten Takes a Public Stand

But James Forten was of different stamp. As he climbed upward on the economic ladder, he gave increasing attention to the nation's most unpopular crusade—that of abolitionism. His religious connections first directed his attention to the need for reform; in 1800 he signed a petition circulated by two Philadelphia ministers asking Congress to modify the Fugitive Slave Act of 1793 and to adopt "such measures as shall in due course emancipate the whole of their brethren from their present situation." As a petitioner, Forten watched with disgust while congressmen rejected the request, then ruled that such petitions had a "tendency to create disquiet and jealousy, and ought therefore to receive no encouragement or countenance from this House." When this resolution was passed by a thumping vote of eighty-five to one, Forten consoled himself by writing the lone champion of the Negroes' cause; but from that date he was determined to do everything in his power to change the attitude of his unsympathetic countrymen.

Forten's first opportunity came in 1813, when the Pennsylvania legislature was debating a bill to ban the entrance of free Negroes into the state. James Forten's attack on this measure was voiced through five letters published in pamphlet form. "Has the God," he asked, "who made the white man and the black, left any record declaring us a different species. Are we not sustained by the same power, supported by the same food, hurt by the same wounds, wounded by the same wrongs, pleased with the same delights, and propagated by the same means. And should we not then enjoy the same liberty, and be protected by the same laws." The legislators, he hoped, "who have hitherto guarded their fellow creatures, without regard to the colour of their skin, will still stretch forth the wings of protection to that race, whose persons have been the scorn, and whose calamities have been the jest of the world for ages."

The Colonization Controversy

The importance of Forten's views cannot be overestimated. Unlike most reformers of that day, he was convinced that no biological difference distinguished Negroes from whites. In this conviction he not only anticipated the basic concept of abolitionism but challenged the contentions of every antislavery leader of his own day. To these humanitarians, whose philosophy was voiced through the American Colonization Society, the Negro was fit only for the barbarism of Africa or the servile life of an American slave. Knowing that slavery was wrong, they planned to win freedom for the Negroes, who would then be sent to Liberia at the Society's expense. Many liberal Northerners embraced colonization, but James Forten refused to be misled. Believing unalterably in the equality of the races, he clung tenaciously to the stand later popularized by William Lloyd Garrison and Theodore Dwight Weld; the slaves should be freed, he held, then educated to take their place in American society. These views stamp Forten as one of the first true abolitionists in the United States.

Forten's opposition to the principles of the American Colonization Society was first voiced in 1817, when its leaders, recognizing his influence among Philadelphia Negroes, asked him to endorse their program. They dangled a tempting bait before him; a man of his prestige, they said, would doubtless become the ruler of Liberia if he cast his lot with them. Forten refused to be tempted. He would, he reputedly told them, "rather remain as James Forten, sail-maker, in Philadelphia, than enjoy the highest offices in the gift of their society." But mere refusal was not enough; his countrymen must be warned of this insidious plot that would eventually drive all Negroes from their adopted land. With this in mind, Forten sought the support of the Reverend Richard Allen, Absalom Jones, Robert Douglass, and others prominent in Philadelphia's Negro society, and with them planned a protest meeting at the Bethel Church. When the group assembled in January, 1817, with Forten in the chair, stirring resolutions were unanimously adopted:

> Whereas, our ancestors (not of choice) were the first successful cultivators of the wilds of America, we, their descendants, feel ourselves entitled to participate in the blessings of her luxuriant soil, which their blood and sweat enriched; and that any measure or system of measures, having a tendency to banish us from her bosom, would not only be cruel, but in direct violation of those principles which have been the boast of this republic.

> *Resolved*, That we view with deep abhorrence the unmerited stigma attempted to be cast upon the reputation of the free people of color by the prompters of this measure, 'that they are a dangerous and useless part of the community,' when, in the state of disfranchisement in which they live, in the hour of danger they ceased to remember their wrongs, and rallied around the standard of their country.

> *Resolved*, That we will never separate ourselves voluntarily from the slave population of this country; they are our brethren by the ties of consanguinity, suffering, and wrong; and we feel there is more virtue in suffering privations with them, than fancied advantages for a season.

> *Resolved*, That without arts, without science, or a proper knowledge of government, to cast into the savage wilds of Africa the free people of color, seems

to us the circuitous route by which they must return to perpetual bondage.

Resolved, That, having the strongest confidence in the justice of God and the philanthropy of the free states, we cheerfully submit our destinies to the guidance of Him who suffers not a sparrow to fall without His special providence.

When the colonizers, undeterred by these protests, prepared to launch a Philadelphia auxiliary of the American Colonization Society during the summer of 1817, Forten was again responsible for a protest meeting, which assembled three thousand strong at the Green Court schoolhouse on August 10. After the usual parade of speakers, an "Address to the humane and benevolent Inhabitants of the city and county of Philadelphia" was unanimously adopted. Arguing that colonization would deprive the freed slaves of the benefits of civilization and religious instruction, this able document from Forten's pen insisted that Liberia would soon be "the abode of every vice, and the home of every misery." Moreover, it would raise the price of slaves still in bondage until masters would be unwilling to grant them freedom. "Let not a purpose be assisted which will stay the cause of the entire abolition of slavery," the address concluded, "and which may defeat it altogether; which proffers to those who do not ask for them *benefits,* but which they consider *injuries,* and which must insure to the multitudes, whose prayers can only reach through us, *misery, sufferings, and perpetual slavery.*"

Impact and Leadership
From that time until his death Forten spared no efforts to reveal the true nature of colonization to his countrymen, both white and Negro. Two years later, in November, 1819, he again presided over a large meeting,

which resolved "That the people of color of Philadelphia now enter and proclaim their most solemn protest against the proposition to send their people to Africa, and against every measure which may have a tendency to convey the idea that they give the project a single particle of countenance or encouragement." Forten was also primarily responsible for a national convention of Negroes which met at Philadelphia on September 15, 1830, to oppose colonization. Similar gatherings were held yearly thereafter, always with James Forten in a leading role. His influence, as much as any other, was responsible for the opposition of Northern Negroes to the American Colonization Society.

The mellowing influence of age did not modify Forten's views on colonization. In 1833, when nearly sixty years of age, he still spoke with the fire of youth when a visitor asked his views on the subject: "My great-grandfather was brought to this country a slave from Africa. My grandfather obtained his own freedom. My father never wore the yoke. He rendered valuable service to his country in the war of our Revolution; and I, though then a boy, was a drummer in that war. I was taken prisoner, and was made to suffer not a little on board the Jersey prison-ship. I have since lived and labored in a useful employment, have acquired property, and have paid taxes in this city. Here I have dwelt until I am nearly sixty years of age, and have brought up and educated a family, as you see, thus far. Yet some ingenious gentlemen have recently discovered that I am still an African; that a continent, three thousand miles, and more, from the place where I was born, is my native country. And I am advised to go home. Well, it may be so. Perhaps if I should only be set on the shore of that distant land, I should recognize all I might see there, and run at once to the old hut where my forefathers lived a hundred years ago."

Forten and William Lloyd Garrison

James Forten's opposition to the American Colonization Society had important results for both himself and
his country. His stout advocacy of racial equality helped
convince William Lloyd Garrison that colonization
was an evil, thus laying the basis for the rise of abolitionism. This, in turn, gave Forten an outlet for his re-
forming zeal; he threw himself into the Garrisonian
crusade with an energy that belied both his advancing
years and his social position.

For by the 1830's, when the antislavery movement
hit its stride, Forten was a man of substance. His pros-
perous sailmaking shop, where he presided over a force
of forty workers, both white and Negro, had allowed
him to amass a fortune of over $100,000 by 1832. This
he used to "live in as handsome a style an anyone could
wish to live." Gathered in his spacious home on Lombard Street were his wife, his eight children, and other
relatives; at times no less than twenty-two persons assembled about the family board. A man of "command-
ing mind and well informed," he was respected by
whites and Negroes alike, largely because of the high
moral principles to which he dedicated his life. He
never drank, and he was a steadfast supporter of temperance societies as well as of organizations advocating
universal peace and women's rights. Forten was also the
guiding spirit behind the American Moral Reform Society, an agency of Negro men dedicated to the "pro-
motion of Education, Temperance, Economy, and Universal Liberty." As founder and perennial president of
the society, he labored effectively to better the stan-
dards of free Negroes throughout the nation.

All this comfort Forten was willing to sacrifice. Knowing that mobs might damage his property or threaten his
aged limbs, he still showed no hesitation when the banner of abolitionism was unfurled by William Lloyd Gar-

rison. To him the Boston reformer was "a chosen instrument, in the Divine hand, to accomplish the great work of the abolition of American slavery," and he must be aided no matter what the cost. Even before the first issue of [Garrison's abolitionist newspaper] *The Liberator* appeared, Forten was soliciting subscriptions among Philadelphia Negroes; by December 31, 1830, he could forward money from twenty-seven subscribers, together with a word of encouragement. "I hope your efforts may not be in vain," he wrote; "and that 'The Liberator' be the means of exposing more and more of the odious system of Slavery, and of raising up friends to the oppressed and degraded People of Colour, throughout the Union. Whilst so much is doing in the world, to ameliorate the condition of mankind, and the spirit of Freedom is marching with rapid strides, and causing tryants to tremble; may America wake from the apathy in which she has long slumbered. She must sooner or later, fall in with the irresistable current!"

Forten's enthusiasm mounted with the actual appearance of *The Liberator*, on January 1, 1831. A month later he sent Garrison twenty more subscriptions; two months later he staged a mass meeting to arouse interest in the cause. But he did not solicit support from others alone; his own coffers were so generously opened that only the wealthy New York merchants, Arthur and Lewis Tappan, contributed more to abolitionism than he did. His only reward was to observe the spreading support for Garrisonianism. "It has," he wrote jubilantly during the spring of 1831, "roused up a spirit in our young people, that has been slumbering for years, and we shall produce writers able to vindicate our cause." Garrison, in turn, developed a warm affection for "the greatly esteemed and venerated sail-maker of Philadelphia," as he called Forten. Seldom did he visit Philadelphia without making his headquarters in the Lombard

Street house. "Such visits," wrote the elderly Forten on one occasion, "are cheering, they are as green spots in the journey of life."

An Abolitionist Hero

His contacts with Garrison allowed Forten to play a significant role in the American Anti-Slavery Society. His house was a regular meeting place for those who gathered to launch the society in the winter of 1833, and he himself served frequently on the Board of Managers, solicited subscriptions for *The Liberator*, and occasionally provided funds when the paper was in financial difficulties. Little wonder that the Society's members in 1840 lauded him with a heart-warming verse that noted his opposition to colonization:

> James Forten, right well
> I love to hear tell
> Of thy aid in our much boasted war;
> And mark with what scorn
> Does thy noble heart spurn
> The friends of Liberia's shore
> James Forten!
> The friends of Liberia's shore.

National acclaim did not dim Forten's interest in the local aspects of abolitionism. Time and again he arranged mass meetings to press for emancipation or to demand equality for the races; time and again he circulated petitions to the state or national legislatures asking protection for runaway slaves or the abolition of bonded servitude. "Let our motto be," he advised the state lawmakers in 1836, "the Law Knows No Distinction." His prominent local position allowed him to serve as delegate to numerous state gatherings, such as that held in Harrisburg in 1837 to urge the end of slavery and colonization.

Only death ended James Forten's crusade. In the fall

of 1841 he was forced to write Garrison that ill health would keep him from active labor in the future, but that his interest in abolitionism was as firm, as ardent, and as undiminished as ever; a year later he died, at the ripe age of seventy-six. His funeral, on February 24, 1842, was one of the largest in the history of Philadelphia. Marching in the procession that escorted his body to the grave were several thousand Negroes and several hundred whites; and men and women of both races paid tribute to his memory in a public gathering that followed. James Forten passed from the scene while the cause that he advocated was still in its infancy, but he left behind him five sons and daughters ready to carry the standard that he had unfurled.

Richard Allen and the First Black Church in America

Richard Newman and Marcia Sawyer

Minister Richard Allen (1760–1831) founded the African Methodist Episcopal (AME) Church in 1816, the first black Christian church in the United States. He was also among the first important and influential black leaders in postcolonial America. In challenging racial segregation in the house of God, Allen (along with his colleague Absalom Jones) helped establish the importance of black churches for the African American community in the antebellum North. The AME Church, and those that followed it, provided not only moral guidance and spiritual edification for its members but also a social network and political meetinghouse. Black churches and religious societies thus served to strengthen burgeoning communities and encourage social and political activism. The following selection, by Richard Newman and Marcia Sawyer, profiles Allen and discusses his central role in bringing the AME Church into existence.

Richard Newman is the fellows and research officer at the Harvard University's W.E.B. Du Bois Institute for Afro-American Research. He has published widely on African American studies. Marcia Sawyer is associate professor of social history and multicultural studies at California State University, San Marcos.

❧   ❧   ❧

Richard Allen founded and became the first bishop of the African Methodist Episcopal (AME) Church, the first black religious denomination. Allen was born in Philadelphia, Pennsylvania, on February 14, 1760, to a family enslaved by Benjamin Chew, a prominent lawyer, attorney general, and judge. Chew sold the family to an owner named Stockley, whom Allen considered kindly, except Stockley sold off Allen's mother and three of his brothers and sisters, and he never saw or heard from any of them again.

Allen's Religious Conversion

Allen was converted to evangelical Protestantism at age seventeen by a Methodist circuit rider. He became a lifelong Methodist in doctrine, adhering to the Wesleyan belief, in contrast to Calvinism, that men and women could play a role in their own salvation. He adhered, also, to early American Methodism's antislavery stance, though within the white churches this was a position that became severely compromised over the years. A white Methodist evangelist named Freeborn Garretson so moved Allen's owner that he agreed to let Allen buy his freedom—for $2,000.

Allen became an itinerant Methodist lay preacher himself, and may have been present at the historic Christmas Conference of 1784, when American Methodism separated from the Church of England, where it had been an internal evangelical party. Allen preached at St. George's Church, Philadelphia, a racially mixed congregation, and he brought in many new black members. The African Americans requested their own separate church, but were refused. They contributed, therefore, to renovating St. George's to make it large enough to accommodate the new members.

Segregation Leads to the First Black Church

In November 1787, the first Sunday in the new building, the black members found themselves segregated in the balcony. Even here, Allen was astonished to see his friend and colleague Absalom Jones dragged to his feet by an usher during prayer and ordered to leave. Outraged, the black members of St. George's walked out of the service, out of the building, and out of a white-controlled Methodist church. Allen and Jones had already formed the Free African Society, which they intended to turn into a nondenominational church, but many were so disgusted by the Methodists that they constituted themselves as St. Thomas Episcopal Church in 1804 under Jones, who became the first black Episcopal minister.

Allen, however, remained true to Methodist theology and polity. To establish a new house of worship, he moved a building that had housed a blacksmith shop to a lot he owned on the corner of Sixth and Lombard streets. Bishop Francis Asbury dedicated it as a Methodist church on July 29, 1794. In 1799 Allen was ordained deacon. Meanwhile, the black Methodists discovered they had been cheated out of their autonomy by the whites of St. George's, but through a lawsuit they eventually managed to regain control of their property in 1807. On April 9, 1816, a conference was organized which included Daniel Coker of Baltimore and other independent black Methodists. Allen was elected bishop of the new group on April 11, and Jones was among the consecrators.

Allen and the African Methodist Episcopal Church immediately became a center of black institutional life. They supported schools and *Freedom's Journal*, they opposed the Colonization Society, and they petitioned legislatures for an end to slavery. Denmark Vesey's slave uprising in Charleston was planned around the AME Church. The vital place and historic role of African Methodism is summarized in Allen's understatement, "The only place blacks felt they could maintain an element of self-expression was the church."

A Christian View of Slavery

Richard Allen

Like Frederick Douglass after him, Richard Allen was a powerful orator, and his sermons expressed his profound faith in the loving and merciful God of the New Testament along with his passionate conviction that slavery was a sin against the Almighty as well as against his fellow black Americans. Although many defenders of slavery also employed Scripture in defense of human bondage, in the following selection from his memoir Allen argues that the Bible's references to slavery served to demonstrate its venality. He warns slaveholders of God's inevitable punishment, but also exhorts slaves to be patient and kind even toward their oppressors since such forbearance may, at best, further the cause of emancipation and, at worst, earn the slave the special pity and mercy of God.

🐝 🐝 🐝

To those who keep slaves, and approve the practice.

The judicious part of mankind, will think it unreasonable, that a superior good conduct is looked for

Richard Allen, *The Life, Experience, and Gospel Labours of the Rt. Reverend Richard Allen, to Which Is Annexed the Rise and Progress of the African Methodist Episcopal Church in the United States of America. Containing a Narrative of the Yellow Fever in the Year of Our Lord 1793: With an Address to the People of Colour in the United States*. Philadelphia: Martin & Boden, 1833.

from our race, by those who stigmatize us as men, whose baseness is incurable, and may therefore be held in a state of servitude, that a merciful man would not doom a beast to; yet you try what you can, to prevent our rising from a state of barbarism you represent us to be in, but we can tell you from a degree of experience, that a black man, although reduced to the most abject state human nature is capable of, short of real madness, can think, reflect, and feel injuries, although it may not be with the same degree of keen resentment and revenge, that you who have been, and are our great oppressors would manifest, if reduced to the pitiable condition of a slave. We believe if you would try the experiment of taking a few black children, and cultivate their minds with the same care, and let them have the same prospect in view as to living in the world, as you would wish for your own children, you would find upon the trial, they were not inferior in mental endowments. I do not wish to make you angry, but excite attention to consider how hateful slavery is, in the sight of that God who hath destroyed kings and princes, for their oppression of the poor slaves. Pharoah and his princes with the posterity of king Saul, were destroyed by the protector and avenger of slaves. Would you not suppose the Israelites to be utterly unfit for freedom, and that it was impossible for them, to obtain to any degree of excellence? Their history shews how slavery had debased their spirits. Men must be wilfully blind, and extremely partial, that cannot see the contrary effects of liberty and slavery upon the mind of man; I truly confess the vile habits often acquired in a state of servitude, are not easily thrown off; the example of the Israelites shews, who with all that Moses could do to reclaim them from it, still continued in their habits more or less; and why will you look for better from us, why will you look for grapes from thorns, or figs from thistles? it is in our posterity enjoying the same privileges with your own, that you ought to look for better things.

When you are pleaded with, do not you reply as Pharoah did, "Wherefore do ye Moses and Aaron let the people from their work, behold the people of the land now are many, and you make them rest from their burthens." We wish you to consider, that God himself was the first pleader of the cause of slaves.

Biblical Words for Slaves and Masters
That God who knows the hearts of all men, and the propensity of a slave to hate this oppressor, hath strictly forbidden it to his chosen people, "Thou shalt not abhor an Egyptian, because thou wast a stranger in his land." Deut. 23. 7. The meek and humble Jesus, the great pattern of humanity, and every other virtue that can adorn and dignify men, hath commanded to love our enemies, to do good to them that hate and despitefully use us. I feel the obligations, I wish to impress them on the minds of our coloured brethren, and that we may all forgive you, as we wish to be forgiven, we think it a great mercy to have all anger and bitterness removed from our minds; I appeal to your own feelings, if it is not very disquieting to feel yourselves under dominion of wrathful disposition.

If you love your children, if you love your country, if you love the God of love, clear your hands from slaves, burthen not your children or your country with them, my heart has been sorry for the blood shed of the oppressors, as well as the oppressed, both appear guilty of each others blood, in the sight of him who hath said, he that sheddeth man's blood, by man shall his blood be shed.

Will you, because you have reduced us to the unhappy condition our colour is in, plead our incapacity for freedom, and our contented condition under oppression, as a sufficient cause for keeping us under the grevious yoke. I have shown the cause,—I will also shew why they appear contented as they can in your sight, but the dreadful insurrections they have made when opportunity has offered, is enough to convince a reasonable man, that great uneasiness and not contentment, is the inhabitant of their hearts. God himself hath pleaded their cause, he hath from time to time raised up instruments for that purpose, sometimes mean and contemptible in your sight, at other times he hath used such as it hath pleased him, with whom you have not thought it beneath your dignity to contend. Many have been convinced of their error, condemned their former conduct, and become zealous advocates for the cause of those, whom you will not suffer to plead for themselves.

To the People of Colour

Feeling an engagement of mind for your welfare, I address you with an affectionate sympathy, having been a slave, and as desirous of freedom as any of you; yet the bands of bondage were so strong that no way appeared for my release; yet at times a hope arose in my heart that a way would open for it; and when my mind was mercifully visited with the feeling of the love of God, then these hopes increased, and a confidence arose that he would make way for my enlargement; and as a patient waiting was necessary, I was sometimes favoured with it; at other times I was very impatient. Then the prospect of liberty almost vanished away, and I was in darkness and perplexity.

I mention experience to you, that your hearts may not sink at the discouraging prospects you may have, and that you may put your trust in God, who sees your condition; and as a merciful father pitieth his children, so doth God pity them that love him; and as your hearts are inclined to serve God, you will feel an affectionate regard towards your masters and mistresses, so called, and the whole family in which you live. This will be seen by them, and tend to promote your liberty, especially with such as have feeling masters; and if they are otherwise, you will have the favour and love of God dwelling in your hearts, which you will value more than any thing else, which will be a consolation in the worst condition you can be in, and no master can deprive you of it, and as life is short and uncertain, and the chief end of our having a being in this world is to be prepared for a better, I wish you to think of this more than any thing else; then you will have a view of that freedom which the sons of God enjoy; and if the troubles of your condition end with your lives, you will be admitted to the freedom which God hath prepared for those of all colours that love him. Here the power of the roost cruel master ends, and all sorrow and fears are wiped away.

The Responsibilities of Freedom

To you who are favoured with freedom—let your conduct manifest your gratitude toward the compassionate masters who have set you free; and let no rancour or ill-will lodge in your breast for any bad treatment you may have received from any. If you do, you transgress against God, who will not hold you guiltless. He would not suffer it even in his beloved people Israel; and you think he will allow it unto us? Many of the white people have been instruments in the hands of God for our good; even such as have held us in captivity, are now pleading our cause with earnestness and zeal; and I am sorry to say, that too many think more of the evil than of the good they have received, and instead of taking the advice of their friends, turn from it with indifference. Much depends upon us for the help of our colour—more than many are aware. If we are lazy and idle, the enemies of freedom plead it as a cause why we ought not to be free, and say we are better in a state of servitude, and that giving us our liberty would be an injury to us, and by such conduct we strengthen the bands of oppression, and keep many in bondage who are more worthy than ourselves. I entreat you to consider the obligations we lie under to help forward the cause of freedom. We who know how bitter the cup is of which the slave hath to drink, O how ought we to feel for those who yet remain in bondage! will even our friends excuse—will God pardon us—for the part we act in making strong the hands of the enemies of our colour?

A Short Address to the Friends of Him Who Hath No Helper

I feel an inexpressible gratitude towards you who have engaged in the cause of the African race; you have wrought a deliverance for many from more than Egyptian bondage; your labours are unremitted for their complete redemption from the cruel subjection they are in. You feel our afflictions—you sympathize with us in the heart-rending distress, when the husband is separated from the wife, and the parents from the children, who are never more to meet in this world. The tear of sensibility trickles from your eye to see the sufferings that keep us from increasing. Your righteous indignation is roused at the means taken to supply the place of the murdered babe; you see our race more effectually destroyed than was in Pharaoh's power to effect upon Israel's sons; you blow the trumpet against the mighty evil; you make the tyrants tremble; you strive to raise the slave to the dignity of a man; you take our children by the hand to lead them in the path of virtue, by your care of our education; you are not ashamed to call the most abject of our race brethren, children of one Father, who hath made of one blood all the nations of the earth. You ask for this, nothing for yourselves, nothing but what is worthy the cause you are engaged in; nothing but that we would be friends to ourselves, and not strengthen the bands of oppression by an evil conduct, when led out of the house of bondage. May He who hath arisen to plead our cause, and engaged you as volunteers in the service, add to your numbers, until the princes shall come forth from Egypt, and Ethiopia stretch out her hands unto God.

David Walker

Robert L. Johns

David Walker (1785–1830) was among the first black abolitionists to be commonly considered a "radical," demanding
immediate emancipation and full civil rights for African
Americans. As historian Eric Foner has observed, before
the 1830s, opponents of slavery generally adopted a less
confrontational stance, seeming to accept the notion of
gradual emancipation and often advocating colonization in
Africa or the Caribbean rather than social and political integration in the United States. Although himself freeborn
in North Carolina, Walker was outraged by the oppression
of enslaved blacks throughout the South. He eventually
settled in Boston, which would become a hub for the abolitionist movement. The following biographical sketch by
Robert L. Johns acknowledges that although relatively little
is known about Walker's life, his contribution to the burgeoning black abolitionist movement—especially in rejecting the notion of colonization—was notable.

   Robert L. Johns is coeditor (with Jessie Carney Smith
and Caspar L. Jordan) of *Black Firsts: 2,000 Years of Extraordinary Achievement* (1994) and (with Jessie Carney Smith)
Statistical Record of Black America (1995).

The life of David Walker was very short and imperfectly recorded. Little suggests that he was destined for widespread fame until he published and distributed a protest work in 1829. This act made him famous in his time, and his small book has resonance down to the present day.

Walker was born on September 28, probably in 1796 or 1797. The brief history of his life in Henry Highland Garnet's 1848 edition of Walker's *Appeal to the Colored Citizens of the World* gives 1785 as the year of Walker's birth, but also states that he died at the age of 34. Recent researchers are inclined to believe that the given age at death is correct. Walker was born in Wilmington, North Carolina, the son of a slave father and a free mother. His mother's status meant that he was also free. His father died before he was born.

Nothing is known of his early life except that Walker developed a hatred of slavery and decided to leave the South. According to his own statements, he then traveled over much of the South and the West, which in his days meant as far as Tennessee. He mentioned two events from that period in the *Appeal*—reading two articles in a Southern newspaper and visiting a Methodist camp meeting near Charleston—that seem to place him in Charleston in 1821. This opens the possibility that he was in contact with Denmark Vesey, a fellow free black, a fellow Methodist, and chief planner of a slave insurrection discovered just before it was to begin the following summer. This contact must remain unproven, however, since Walker's name occurs nowhere in the documents about the revolt. It is also possible that he spent some time in Philadelphia before settling in Boston.

In 1825 Walker established himself in Boston; his name appeared in the city directory, where he was listed as a clothes dealer at the City Market. In 1828 his place of business was at 20 Brattle Street, and he moved the following year to number 40 in the same street. He operated a new and used clothing store. In 1828 he and two other used-clothes dealers were charged with receiving stolen goods and tried. However, all three kept good records and were acquitted because they could show that they had accepted the items in good faith.

Beginning in 1827 Walker resided on Belknap Street (now Joy Street). He was a faithful member of the May Street Methodist Church, which was organized under black exhorter Samuel Snowden in 1818 and acquired its first permanent building on May Street in 1823. Snowden and the Baptist minister, Thomas Paul, were the only two black ministers in Boston. (Although Walker expressed great admiration of Richard Allen, the African Methodists did not have a church in Boston until 1833.)

Walker quickly began to make his mark in the Boston African American community. He was active in the Massachusetts General Colored Association, an early black organization devoted to abolition of slavery and to full equality. In his mind this association was a nucleus for a national mass organization of all blacks. Along with Thomas Paul, Walker was one of the two agents in Boston of *Freedom's Journal*, the first black newspaper, which began publication at the end of March 1827. One of Walker's speeches before the General Colored Association appeared in the paper on December 19, 1828. As reprinted . . . in *David Walker's Appeal*, Walker was already sounding the theme of the *Appeal*:

> Shall we keep slumbering on, with our arms completely folded up, exclaiming every now and then, against our miseries, yet never do the least thing to ameliorate our condition, or that of posterity? . . . Ought we not to form ourselves into a general body,

to protect, aid, and assist each other to the utmost of our power . . . ?

In 1828 Walker married Eliza. It has been suggested that Garnet's omission of her maiden name in his account of Walker's life may indicate that she was a fugitive slave. A daughter was born to the couple, but she died of lung fever just a few days before her father. Walker's only surviving child, Edwin (1831?—1910), later one of the first two blacks elected to the Massachusetts legislature in 1866, was born posthumously.

According to Garnet, Walker was "prepossessing, being six feet in height, slender and well proportioned. His hair was loose, and his complexion dark." He was militant and courageous. When friends urged him to flee to Canada after the storm raised by his tract, he replied, according to Garnet, "I will stand my ground. *Somebody must die in this cause.* I may be doomed to the stake and to the fire, or to the scaffold tree, but it is not in me to falter if I can promote the work of emancipation."

Walker assured his fame by publishing *Appeal, in Four Articles, Together with a Preamble to the Colored Citizens of the World, But in Particular, and Very Expressly to Those of the United States of America.* The title page carried the date of September 28, 1829. Although this was the third protest published by an African American in 1829—George Moses Horton, a North Carolina slave poet had published some stanzas on freedom and Robert Alexander Young's *Ethiopian Manifesto* had appeared a short time earlier—it caused consternation in the South, where the first copies arrived before the end of the year. The third edition of the *Appeal* with more revisions and additions appeared in June 1830.

One of the reasons for the resonance of the *Appeal* was its effective distribution. Walker took steps to see that it reached the South. Tantalizing hints, again falling short of proof, imply that the distribution may have been more systematically organized than we can now know. Of the copies distributed by individuals and not mailed, many appear to have gone by ship. Copies have been discovered in Savannah, Georgia; Charleston, South Carolina; Richmond, Virginia; New Orleans, Louisiana; and several cities in North Carolina. Some white men living in the region were involved. Elijah H. Burritt, a white printer in Milledgeville, Georgia, was forced to flee because he had obtained copies of the work for distribution. The alarm was general in the South, and state legislatures passed laws against seditious publications. In the North, rumors claimed that Southerners were offering $3,000 for Walker dead and $10,000 for him alive in the South.

Walker died suddenly on August 3, 1830, at his home. On January 22, 1831, the *Liberator*, a militant anti-slavery weekly newspaper edited by William Lloyd Garrison, published a letter from "A Colored Bostonian," alleging that Walker had perished at the hands of slaveholders. Apparently many blacks in Boston believed this to be true, but there is no convincing evidence that the death was not natural. There probably now exists no evidence to prove decisively either conclusion.

Walker's *Appeal* offers a convenient date for the beginning of the sectional hostility that culminated in the Civil War. The South began to move toward white solidarity on the issue of slavery; the North saw the beginnings of the abolitionist movement, which would slowly overcome that region's indifference to the issue. William Lloyd Garrison, who began publishing the *Liberator* in 1830, was influenced by Walker although he could not agree with him on all points. In turn, Walker's son bore Garrison as a middle name. Generations of black militants beginning with Henry Highland Garnet, who republished the *Appeal* in 1848, have found inspiration in Walker's work.

An Appeal to Resistance

David Walker

David Walker issued his *Appeal . . . to the Coloured Citizens of the World, but in Particular, and Very Expressly, to Those of the United States of America* in 1829, from which the following selection is an excerpt. Like Richard Allen and Frederick Douglass, Walker questions the Christian piety of a people who would endorse slavery. He also castigates Thomas Jefferson, who was notoriously ambivalent about slavery. Ultimately, what may be most remarkable about Walker's *Appeal* are his rejection of conciliation or persuasion as instruments of emancipation and his insistence that rather than immigrating to Haiti or Europe, blacks have a right to U.S. citizenship by virtue of their labor in building the country. Walker all but dares white Americans either to give blacks their rightful freedom or else be prepared for violent resistance.

🐝 🐝 🐝

*M*y dearly beloved Brethren and Fellow Citizens.
  Having travelled over a considerable portion of these United States, and having, in the course of my travels,

taken the most accurate observations of things as they exist—the result of my observations has warranted the full and unshaken conviction, that we, (coloured people of these United States,) are the most degraded, wretched, and abject set of beings that ever lived since the world began; and I pray God that none like us ever may live again until time shall be no more. They tell us of the Israelites in Egypt, the Helots in Sparta, and of the Roman Slaves, which last were made up from almost every nation under heaven, whose sufferings under those ancient and heathen nations, were, in comparison with ours, under this enlightened and Christian nation, no more than a cypher—or, in other words, those heathen nations of antiquity, had but little more among them than the name and form of slavery; while wretchedness and endless miseries were reserved, apparently in a phial, to be poured out upon, our fathers, ourselves and our children, by *Christian* Americans! . . .

American Christians Are More Wicked than Egyptians

I call upon the professing Christians, I call upon the philanthropist, I call upon the very tyrant himself, to show me a page of history, either sacred or profane, on which a verse can be found, which maintains, that the Egyptians heaped the *insupportable insult* upon the children of Israel, by telling them that they were not of the *human family*. Can the whites deny this charge? Have they not, after having reduced us to the deplorable condition of slaves under their feet, held us up as descending originally from the tribes of *Monkeys* or *Orang-Outangs*? O! my God! I appeal to every man of feeling— is not this insupportable? Is it not heaping the most gross insult upon our miseries, because they have got us under their feet and we cannot help ourselves? Oh! pity us we pray thee, Lord Jesus, Master.—Has Mr. [Thomas] Jefferson declared to the world, that we are inferior to the whites, both in the endowments of our bodies and our minds? It is indeed surprising, that a man of such great learning, combined with such excellent natural parts, should speak so of a set of men in chains. I do not know what to compare it to, unless, like putting one wild deer in an iron cage, where it will be secured, and hold another by the side of the same, then let it go, and expect the one in the cage to run as fast as the one at liberty. So far, my brethren, were the Egyptians from heaping these insults upon their slaves, that Pharaoh's daughter took Moses, a son of Israel for her own. . . .

Jefferson's Ideas About Slavery Are Wrong

The world knows, that slavery as it existed [among the Romans] was . . . (which was the primary cause of their destruction) . . . comparatively speaking, no more than a *cypher*, when compared with ours under the Americans. Indeed I should not have noticed the Roman slaves, had not the very learned and penetrating Mr. Jefferson said, "when a master was murdered, all his slaves in the same house, or within hearing, were condemned to death."—Here let me ask Mr. Jefferson, (but he is gone to answer at the bar of God, for the deeds done in his body while living,) I therefore ask the whole American people, had I not rather die, or be put to death, than to be a slave to any tyrant, who takes not only my own, but my wife and children's lives by the inches? Yea, would I meet death with avidity far! far!! in preference to such *servile submission* to the murderous hands of tyrants. Mr. Jefferson's very severe remarks on us have been so extensively argued upon by men whose attainments in literature, I shall never be able to reach, that I would not have meddled with it, were it not to solicit each of my brethren, who has the spirit of a man, to buy a copy of Mr. Jefferson's "Notes on Virginia," and put it in the hand of his son. . . .

But let us review Mr. Jefferson's remarks respecting us some further. Comparing our miserable fathers, with the learned philosophers of Greece, he says: "Yet notwithstanding these and other discouraging circumstances among the Romans, their slaves were often their rarest artists. They excelled too, in science, insomuch as to be usually employed as tutors to their master's children, Epictetus [Greek philosopher], Terence and Phaedrus [Roman poets], were slaves,—but they were of the race of whites. It is not their *condition* then, but *nature*, which has produced the distinction." See this, my brethren!! Do you believe that this assertion is swallowed by millions of the whites? Do you know that Mr. Jefferson was one of as great characters as ever lived among the whites? See his writings for the world, and public labours for the United States of America. Do you believe that the assertions of such a man, will pass away into oblivion unobserved by this people and the world? If you do you are much mistaken—See how the American people treat us—have we souls in our bodies? Are we men who have any spirits at all? I know that there are many *swell-bellied* fellows among us, whose greatest object is to fill their stomachs. Such I do not mean—I am after those who know and feel, that we are MEN, as well as other people; to them, I say, that unless we try to refute Mr. Jefferson's arguments respecting us, we will only establish them. . . .

God Created All Men Equal

I must observe to my brethren that at the close of the first Revolution in this country, with Great Britain, there were but thirteen States in the Union, now there are twenty-four, most of which are slave-holding States, and the whites are dragging us around in chains and in handcuffs, to their new States and Territories to work their mines and farms, to enrich them and their children—and millions of them believing firmly that we being a little darker than they, were made by our Creator to be an inheritance to them and their children for ever—the same as a parcel of *brutes*.

Are we MEN!!—I ask you, O my brethren are we MEN? Did our Creator make us to be slaves to dust and ashes like ourselves? Are they not dying worms as well as we? Have they not to make their appearance before the tribunal of Heaven, to answer for the deeds done in the body, as well as we? Have we any other Master but Jesus Christ alone? Is he not their Master as well as ours?—What right then, have we to obey and call any other Master, but Himself? How we could be so *submissive* to a gang of men, whom we cannot tell whether they are as good as ourselves or not, I never could conceive. However, this is shut up with the Lord, and we cannot precisely tell—but I declare, we judge men by their works.

White Hypocrisy

The whites have always been an unjust, jealous, unmerciful, avaricious and blood-thirsty set of beings, always seeking after power and authority. . . .

To my no ordinary astonishment, [a] Reverend gentleman got up and told us (coloured people) that slaves must be obedient to their masters—must do their duty to their masters or be whipped—the whip was made for the backs of fools, &c. Here I pause for a moment, to give the world time to consider what was my surprise, to hear such preaching from a minister of my Master, whose very gospel is that of peace and not of blood and whips, as this pretended preacher tried to make us believe. What the American preachers can think of us, I aver this day before my God, I have never been able to define. They have newspapers and monthly periodicals, which they receive in continual succession, but on the pages of which, you will scarcely ever find a paragraph respecting slavery, which is ten thousand times more injurious to this country than all the other evils put together; and which will be the final overthrow of its government, unless something is very speedily done; for their cup is nearly full.—Perhaps they will laugh at or make light of this; but I tell you Americans! that unless you speedily alter your course, *you* and your *Country are gone!!!!!* . . .

Blacks Owe Whites No Gratitude for Slavery

If any of us see fit to go away, go to those who have been for many years, and are now our greatest earthly friends and benefactors—the English. If not so, go to our brethren, the Haitians, who, according to their word, are bound to protect and comfort us. The Americans say, that we are ungrateful—but I ask them for heaven's sake, what should we be grateful to them for—for murdering our fathers and mothers?—Or do they wish us to return thanks to them for chaining and handcuffing us, branding us, cramming fire down our throats, or for keeping us in slavery, and beating us nearly or quite to death to make us work in ignorance and miseries, to support them and their families. They certainly think that we are a gang of fools. Those among them, who have volunteered their services for our redemption, though we are unable to compensate them for their labours, we nevertheless thank them from the bottom of our hearts, and have our eyes steadfastly fixed upon them, and their labours of love for God and man.—But do slave-holders think that we thank them for keeping us in miseries, and taking our lives by the inches? . . .

Full Citizenship, Not Colonization

Let no man of us budge one step, and let slave-holders come to beat us from our country. America is more our country, than it is the white—we have enriched it with our *blood and tears*. The greatest riches in all America have arisen from our blood and tears:—and will they drive us from our property and homes, which we have earned with our *blood*? They must look sharp or this very thing will bring swift destruction upon them. The Americans have got so fat on our blood and groans, that they have almost forgotten the God of armies. . . .

Do the colonizationists think to send us off without first being reconciled to us? Do they think to bundle us up like brutes and send us off, as they did our brethren of the State of Ohio? Have they not to be reconciled to us, or reconcile us to them, for the cruelties with which they have afflicted our fathers and us? Methinks colonizationists think they have a set of brutes to deal with, sure enough. Do they think to drive us from our country and homes, after having enriched it with our blood and tears, and keep back millions of our dear brethren, sunk in the most barbarous wretchedness, to dig up gold and silver for them and their children? Surely, the Americans must think that we are brutes, as some of them have represented us to be. They think that we do not feel for our brethren, whom they are murdering by the inches, but they are dreadfully deceived. . . .

What nation under heaven, will be able to do any thing with us, unless God gives us up into its hand? But Americans, I declare to you, while you keep us and our children in bondage, and treat us like brutes, to make us support you and your families, we cannot be your friends. You do not look for it do you? Treat us then like men, and we will be your friends. And there is not a doubt in my mind, but that the whole of the past will be sunk into oblivion, and we yet, under God, will become a united and happy people. The whites may say it is impossible, but remember that nothing is impossible with God. . . .

Freedom Is Worth Dying For

I count my life not dear unto me, but I am ready to be offered at any moment, For what is the use of living, when in fact I am dead. But remember, Americans, that as miserable, wretched, degraded and abject as you have made us in preceding, and in this generation, to support you and your families, that some of you, (whites) on the continent of America, will yet curse the day that you ever were born. You want slaves, and want us for your slaves!!! My colour will yet, root some of you out of the very face of the earth!!!!!! You may doubt it if you please. I know that thousands will doubt—they think they have us so well secured in wretchedness, to them and their children, that it is impossible for such things to occur. . . .

See your Declaration, Americans!!! Do you understand your own language? Hear your languages, proclaimed to the world, July 4th, 1776—"We hold these truths to be self evident—that ALL MEN ARE CREATED EQUAL!! that they *are endowed by their Creator with certain unalienable rights;* that among these are life, *liberty,* and the pursuit of happiness!!" Compare your own language above, extracted from your Declaration of Independence, with your cruelties and murders inflicted by your cruel and unmerciful fathers and yourselves on our fathers and on us—men who have never given your fathers or you the least provocation!!!!!

CHAPTER

2

Profiles · in · History

Frederick Douglass: The Voice of Freedom

Frederick Douglass's Life of Leadership

George M. Fredrickson

Frederick Douglass (1817–1895) was the most prominent black abolitionist of his time and among the leading voices of the antislavery movement as a whole. Equally gifted as a writer and an orator, Douglass was a major figure in nineteenth-century American literature as well as in political history. As an abolitionist activist, he disagreed with both William Lloyd Garrison's rejection of the political realm and fellow black abolitionist Henry Highland Garnet's exhortation to violent rebellion; Douglass's ability to blend idealism and pragmatism informed his public life from his first antislavery oration until his death in 1895.

In the following biographical selection, historian George M. Fredrickson chronicles Douglass's escape from slavery and his rise to eminence in the abolitionist movement, including his break with Garrison, who was arguably the most eminent white American antislavery activist. Fredrickson's discussion of Douglass's public life during and after the Civil War is a reminder that for the one-time fugitive slave Frederick Bailey, emancipation was only the first important step toward full equality for black Americans.

George M. Fredrickson, *The Arrogance of Race: Historical Perspectives on Slavery, Racism, and Social Inequality*. Middletown, CT: Wesleyan University Press, 1988.

Frederick Douglass was not only the most famous Afro-American of the nineteenth century; when he died in 1895 he was one of the best-known Americans of any race. A eulogist plausibly compared his international reputation to [Abraham] Lincoln's. No other black leader before Martin Luther King, Jr., was able to appeal to whites on behalf of racial justice and equality with so much force and effect. Part of Douglass's prestige and influence came from his skill with the written and spoken word; he was a great orator at a time when elocution was highly valued and a forceful writer whose three autobiographies (published in 1845, 1855, and 1881) rank with the best written by Americans. But it was more the substance than the style of his autobiographical writings that made him such a remarkable and intriguing figure. At a time when most whites viewed blacks as inherently inferior to themselves, he rose from the depths of slavery to such a height of Victorian eminence that he challenged this prevailing assumption in dramatic fashion. Racists did, however, have a solution to the Douglass problem; they simply attributed his undeniable intelligence and character to his white father.

The Early Years

Douglass was born on the Eastern Shore of Maryland in 1818, the son of a slave woman and an unknown white man (probably his master). Sometimes the slave offspring of white fathers were treated with special consideration, but this does not seem to have been the case with Douglass. His earliest years were spent happily enough at the isolated cabin of his elderly grandmother, but at the age of six he was sent to the great plantation where his master was serving as a steward for one of the largest landowners on the Eastern Shore. There he viewed some of the incidents of brutality that he later recorded in his autobiography; personally, however, he suffered from chronic hunger rather than physical abuse. His greatest deprivation was the loss of a mother he had rarely seen: she died after paying him one brief visit in his new home.

Douglass was saved from a life of plantation drudgery, at least temporarily, when he was consigned to the household of a shipwright in Baltimore. At the shipwright's he received kind treatment, especially from his mistress, who served for a time as a kind of surrogate mother. She started to teach him to read but was induced to give up the effort in the face of strong public sentiment against making slaves literate. Douglass found ways to continue his education surreptitiously. Eventually he came to possess a copy of *The Columbian Orator*, a collection of famous speeches in defense of liberty, which included an attack on black enslavement. From this great source of Enlightenment and American revolutionary rhetoric Douglass derived his basic ideas and the elements of his own oratorical style.

When Douglass was fifteen, a change in his ownership sent him back to a plantation, where he faced the dismal prospect of spending the rest of his life as a field hand. Finding him sullen and resentful because of his altered circumstances, his new master rented him out to a local farmer with a reputation as a "negro breaker." What most readers remember most vividly from Douglass's autobiographical writings are the accounts of his subsequent degradation and his recovery from it by standing up to the Negro-breaker and besting him in a fair fight, thus winning immunity from further punishment.

Such things happened; faced with defiance from valuable slaves who clearly showed that they would rather die than be whipped, masters or overseers sometimes took the path of least resistance and acquiesced. After being returned to his owner and rented out again, Douglass continued on the path of resistance and plotted with other slaves to escape to the North. The conspiracy was uncovered before it could be acted on, and Douglass was thrown in jail. But then he had a most extraordinary piece of good luck: instead of being sold to the deep South—the usual fate of would-be runaways—he was sent back to the shipwright in Baltimore and allowed to become an apprentice artisan.

Although harassed and beaten up by the white apprentices with whom he worked, Douglass learned his trade and was eventually granted the ultimate privilege of skilled slaves—the right to "hire his own time." While working and living independently in return for a weekly payment to his master, he planned his escape. Exactly how he managed it was concealed in his pre–Civil War autobiographies for obvious reasons. As revealed after the war, his escape turned out to have been one of the easiest and least harrowing on record. He simply borrowed some papers indicating free status from a Negro sailor, boarded a train, rode to freedom, and then mailed the papers back to their owner. . . .

A New Name, a New Life

After escaping from slavery and taking a new name to conceal his identity, Douglass became a major figure in the abolitionist movement. He first allied himself with William Lloyd Garrison and the wing of the movement that placed moral purity above political expediency. The Garrisonians refused to vote or hold office and condemned the Constitution as a "covenant with Death" because it seemed to sanction slavery. As the first runaway slave to become an abolitionist orator, Douglass roused a sensation when he told audiences of his personal experiences as a bondsman. Because he was so well spoken, however, there was widespread skepticism as to whether he was really a fugitive. It was partly to prove his authenticity that Douglass wrote his *Narrative of the Life of Frederick Douglass*, thereby putting himself in danger of recapture and extradition because he wrote about specific names and places.

After publishing this masterpiece of antislavery polemic and autobiographical art, he fled to England, returning to the United States only after British well-wishers had arranged to purchase his freedom. For condoning this purchase, and thus seeming to acknowledge the legality of slavery, Douglass was criticized by purists in the American antislavery movement. This reaction contributed to his estrangement from the perfectionist doctrines and paternalistic racial attitudes of the Garrisonians. His intention to follow an independent course was soon revealed when he founded an antislavery newspaper of his own, against the wishes of Garrison and his supporters, who did not welcome a journal that would threaten the preeminence of their own organ. There was more than a hint of race prejudice in the ferocious attacks they leveled at this black man who refused to accept white guidance and leadership. At one point the Garrisonians even spread malicious gossip about Douglass's relationship with a white Englishwoman who assisted him with his paper.

Douglass and Politics

Douglass's independence eventually extended to matters of doctrine; his editorial line gradually shifted from the quasi-anarchism of the Garrisonians toward the "moderate" abolitionist view that political action was justified and that the Constitution could be interpreted as an antislavery document. During the 1850s, Douglass supported efforts to make slavery a national political issue. He rejoiced in the rise and ultimate triumph of the Republican party, even though this new sectional party was committed to stopping the spread of slavery and not to ending it completely. His growing pragmatism and accommodation to gradual change through the political system was strengthened during the war when he supported the Lincoln administration in its halting steps toward emancipation, while at the same time criticizing it for not going faster. Recognizing that Douglass was preeminent among black leaders and a potentially valuable political ally, Lincoln sought his advice and treated him with conspicuous respect. The war and the resulting emancipation solidified Douglass's faith in American values and institutions and made him a lifelong optimist about the prospects for black equality.

Douglass's postwar career was considerably less exciting and heroic than his earlier abolitionist phase. As [biographer Waldo E.] Martin put it, an "activist-reformist" style of leadership was replaced by an "emblematic-patriarchal" mode. Although he continued to protest vigorously against racial discrimination and injustice, his new role as a political insider and stalwart Republican turned him, for most purposes, into a Gilded Age conservative, an exemplar of the black cause through his personal eminence and success rather than through his leadership in mobilizing blacks to struggle for equality. For his loyalty to the Republicans—which persisted even following Reconstruction when the party had in effect deserted southern blacks—he was rewarded with appointments as United States marshal and recorder of deeds for the District of Columbia, and finally, toward the end of his life, as American minister to Haiti. Meager as these patronage rewards may now appear to be, they represented the highest nonelective positions attained by any Afro-American in the nineteenth century.

Slavery Is the Religion of the Land

Frederick Douglass

In the following selection, which served as an appendix to his influential memoir *The Narrative of the Life of Frederick Douglass* (1845), Douglass focuses on one of his most frequent topics: the hypocrisy of the American people, who claim Christian devoutness while supporting slavery. Although Douglass did not favor the violent resistance espoused by radicals such as Henry Highland Garnet, his tone is unmistakably angry as he mocks the avowed religious piety of those who tolerate the evil of slavery. That Douglass castigates northerners as well as southerners is a telling reminder of the fact that the majority of the North did not endorse the abolitionist cause, particularly not in 1845, fifteen years before the secession crisis. Thus, abolitionists struggled against northern complacency as well as southern complicity.

❦ ❦ ❦

Frederick Douglass, *Narrative of the Life of Frederick Douglass: An American Slave Written by Himself.* Boston, MA: Anti-Slavery Office, 1845.

I find, since reading over the foregoing Narrative, that I have, in several instances, spoken in such a tone and manner, respecting religion, as may possibly lead those unacquainted with my religious views to suppose me an opponent of all religion. To remove the liability of such misapprehension, I deem it proper to append the following brief explanation. What I have said respecting and against religion, I mean strictly to apply to the *slaveholding religion* of this land, and with no possible reference to Christianity proper; for, between the Christianity of this land, and the Christianity of Christ, I recognize the widest possible difference—so wide, that to receive the one as good, pure, and holy, is of necessity to reject the other as bad, corrupt, and wicked. To be the friend of the one, is of necessity to be the enemy of the other. I love the pure, peaceable, and impartial Christianity of Christ: I therefore hate the corrupt, slaveholding, women-whipping, cradle-plundering, partial and hypocritical Christianity of this land. Indeed, I can see no reason, but the most deceitful one, for calling the religion of this land Christianity. I look upon it as the climax of all misnomers, the boldest of all frauds, and the grossest of all libels. Never was there a clearer case of "stealing the livery of the court of heaven to serve the devil in." I am filled with unutterable loathing when I contemplate the religious pomp and show, together with the horrible inconsistencies, which every where surround me. We have men-stealers for ministers, women-whippers for missionaries, and cradle-plunderers for church members. The man who wields the blood-clotted cowskin during the week fills the pulpit on Sunday, and claims to be a minister of the meek and lowly Jesus. The man who robs me of my earnings at the end of each week meets me as a class-leader on Sunday morning, to show me the way of life, and the path of salvation. He who sells my sister, for purposes of prostitution, stands forth as the pious advocate of purity. He who proclaims it a religious duty to read the Bible denies me the right of learning to read the name of the God who made me. He who is the religious advocate of marriage robs whole millions of its sacred influence, and leaves them to the ravages of wholesale pollution. The warm defender of the sacredness of the family relation is the same that scatters whole families,—sundering husbands and wives, parents and children, sisters and brothers,—leaving the hut vacant, and the hearth desolate. We see the thief preaching against theft, and the adulterer against adultery. We have men sold to build churches, women sold to support the gospel, and babes sold to purchase Bibles for the *poor heathen! all for the glory of God and the good of souls!* The slave auctioneer's bell and the church-going bell chime in with each other, and the bitter cries of the heart-broken slave are drowned in the religious shouts of his pious master. Revivals of religion and revivals in the slave-trade go hand in hand together. The slave prison and the church stand near each other. The clanking of fetters and the rattling of chains in the prison, and the pious psalm and solemn prayer in the church, may be heard at the same time. The dealers in the bodies and souls of men erect their stand in the presence of the pulpit, and they mutually help each other. The dealer gives his bloodstained gold to support the pulpit, and the pulpit, in return, covers his infernal business with the garb of Christianity. Here we have religion and robbery the allies of each other—devils dressed in angels' robes, and hell presenting the semblance of paradise.

> Just God! and these are they,
> Who minister at thine altar,
> God of right!
> Men who their hands, with prayer and blessing, lay
> On Israel's ark of light.

What! preach, and kidnap men?
Give thanks, and rob thy own afflicted poor?
Talk of thy glorious liberty, and then
Bolt hard the captive's door?

"What! servants of thy own
Merciful Son, who came to seek and save
The homeless and the outcast, fettering down
The tasked and plundered slave!

"Pilate and Herod friends!
Chief priests and rulers, as of old, combine!
Just God and holy! is that church which lends
Strength to the spoiler thine?"

The False Christianity of America

The Christianity of America is a Christianity, of whose votaries it may be as truly said, as it was of the ancient scribes and Pharisees, "They bind heavy burdens, and grievous to be borne, and lay them on men's shoulders, but they themselves will not move them with one of their fingers. All their works they do for to be seen of men.—They love the uppermost rooms at feasts, and the chief seats in the synagogues, . . . and to be called of men, Rabbi, Rabbi.—But woe unto you, scribes and Pharisees, hypocrites! for ye shut up the kingdom of heaven against men; for ye neither go in yourselves, neither suffer ye them that are entering to go in. Ye devour widows' houses, and for a pretense make long prayers; therefore ye shall receive the greater damnation. Ye compass sea and land to make one proselyte, and when he is made, ye make him twofold more the child of hell than yourselves.—Woe unto you, scribes and Pharisees, hypocrites! for ye pay tithe of mint, and anise, and cumin, and have omitted the weightier matters of the law, judgment, mercy, and faith; these ought ye to have done, and not to leave the other undone. Ye blind guides! which strain at a gnat, and swallow a camel. Woe unto you, scribes and Pharisees, hypocrites! for ye make clean the outside of the cup and of the platter; but within, they are full of extortion and excess.—Woe unto you, scribes and Pharisees, hypocrites! for ye are like unto whited sepulchres, which indeed appear beautiful outward, but are within full of dead men's bones, and of all uncleanness. Even so ye also outwardly appear righteous unto men, but within ye are full of hypocrisy and iniquity."

Dark and terrible as is this picture, I hold it to be strictly true of the overwhelming mass of professed Christians in America. They strain at a gnat, and swallow a camel. Could any thing be more true of our churches? They would be shocked at the proposition of fellowshipping a *sheep*-stealer; and at the same time they hug to their communion a *man*-stealer, and brand me with being an infidel, if I find fault with them for it. They attend with Pharisaical strictness to the outward forms of religion, and at the same time neglect the weightier matters of the law, judgment, mercy, and faith. They are always ready to sacrifice, but seldom to show mercy. They are they who are represented as professing to love God whom they have not seen, whilst they hate their brother whom they have seen. They love the heathen on the other side of the globe. They can pray for him, pay money to have the Bible put into his hand, and missionaries to instruct him; while they despise and totally neglect the heathen at their own doors.

Such is, very briefly, my view of the religion of this land; and to avoid any misunderstanding, growing out of the use of general terms, I mean by the religion of this land, that which is revealed in the words, deeds, and actions, of those bodies, north and south, calling themselves Christian churches, and yet in union with slaveholders. It is against religion, as presented by these bodies, that I have felt it my duty to testify.

What Is to the Slave the Fourth of July?

Frederick Douglass

Frederick Douglass's speech "What Is to the Slave the Fourth of July?" was delivered at a meeting of the Rochester Ladies' Anti-Slavery Society on July 5, 1852. Douglass begins by comparing the American struggle for independence against British tyranny with the current situation of the slave. While white America celebrates its emancipation on the Fourth of July, black Americans still suffer under oppression, bondage, and tyranny. The slave is excluded from reaping the fruits of independence. Douglass argues forcefully for the humanity of blacks and their entitlement to liberty. Throughout the speech Douglass characteristically assails white Christians for their hypocrisy, yet he concludes on a note of cautious hope: American endorsement of slavery, increasingly condemned by abolitionists on both sides of the Atlantic, is doomed.

🐝 🐝 🐝

Frederick Douglass, address to the Rochester Ladies' Anti-Slavery Society, Rochester, NY, July 5, 1852.

Fellow citizens, pardon me, and allow me to ask, why am I called upon to speak here today? What have I or those I represent to do with your national independence? Are the great principles of political freedom and of natural justice, embodied in that Declaration of Independence, extended to us? And am I, therefore, called upon to bring our humble offering to the national altar, and to confess the benefits, and express devout gratitude for the blessings resulting from your independence to us?

Would to God, both for your sakes and ours, that an affirmative answer could be truthfully returned to these questions. Then would my task be light, and my burden easy and delightful. For who is there so cold that a nation's sympathy could not warm him? Who so obdurate and dead to the claims of gratitude, that would not thankfully acknowledge such priceless benefits? Who so stolid and selfish that would not give his voice to swell the hallelujahs of a nation's jubilee, when the chains of servitude had been torn from his limbs? I am not that man. In a case like that, the dumb might eloquently speak, and the "lame man leap as an hart."

No Rejoicing for Black Americans

But such is not the state of the case. I say it with a sad sense of disparity between us. I am not included within the pale of this glorious anniversary! Your high independence only reveals the immeasurable distance between us. The blessings in which you this day rejoice are not enjoyed in common. The rich inheritance of justice, liberty, prosperity, and independence bequeathed by your fathers is shared by you, not by me. The sunlight that brought life and healing to you has brought stripes and death to me. This Fourth of July is yours, not mine. You may rejoice, I must mourn. To drag a man in fetters into the grand illuminated temple of liberty, and call upon him to join you in joyous anthems, were inhuman mockery and sacrilegious irony. Do you mean, citizens, to mock me, by asking me to speak today? If so, there is a parallel to your conduct. And let me warn you, that it is dangerous to copy the example of a nation (Babylon) whose crimes, towering up to heaven, were thrown down by the breath of the Almighty, burying that nation in irrecoverable ruin.

Fellow citizens, above your national, tumultuous joy, I hear the mournful wail of millions, whose chains, heavy and grievous yesterday, are today rendered more intolerable by the jubilant shouts that reach them. If I do forget, if I do not remember those bleeding children of sorrow this day, "may my right hand forget her cunning, and may my tongue cleave to the roof of my mouth!"

To forget them, to pass lightly over their wrongs and to chime in with the popular theme would be treason most scandalous and shocking, and would make me a reproach before God and the world.

A Nation's "Great Sin and Shame"

My subject, then, fellow citizens, is "American Slavery." I shall see this day and its popular characteristics from the slave's point of view. Standing here, identified with the American bondman, making his wrongs mine, I do not hesitate to declare, with all my soul, that the character and conduct of this nation never looked blacker to me than on this Fourth of July.

Whether we turn to the declarations of the past, or to the professions of the present, the conduct of the nation seems equally hideous and revolting. America is false to the past, false to the present, and solemnly binds herself to be false to the future. Standing with God and the crushed and bleeding slave on this occasion, I will, in the name of humanity, which is outraged, in the name of liberty, which is fettered, in the name of the Constitution and the Bible, which are disregarded and trampled upon, dare to call in question and to denounce, with all the emphasis I can command, everything that serves to perpetuate slavery—the great sin and shame of America! "I will not equivocate—I will not excuse." I will use the severest language I can command, and yet not one word shall escape me that any man, whose judgment is not blinded by prejudice, or who is not at heart a slave-holder, shall not confess to be right and just.

Slavery, Blacks, and the Law

But I fancy I hear some of my audience say it is just in this circumstance that you and your brother Abolitionists fail to make a favorable impression on the public mind. Would you argue more and denounce less, would you persuade more and rebuke less, your cause would be much more likely to succeed. But, I submit, where all is plain there is nothing to be argued. What point in the anti-slavery creed would you have me argue? On what branch of the subject do the people of this country need light? Must I undertake to prove that the slave is a man? That point is conceded already. Nobody doubts it. The slaver-holders themselves acknowledge it in the enactment of laws for their government. They acknowledge it when they punish disobedience on the part of the slave. There are seventy-two crimes in the State of Virginia, which, if committed by a black man (no matter how ignorant he be), subject him to the punishment of death; while only two of these same crimes will subject a white man to like punishment.

What is this but the acknowledgment that the slave is a moral, intellectual, and responsible being? The manhood of the slave is conceded. It is admitted in the fact that Southern statute books are covered with enactments, forbidding, under severe fines and penalties, the teaching of the slave to read and write. When you can point to any such laws in reference to the beasts of the field, then I may consent to argue the manhood of the slave. When the dogs in your streets, when the fowls of the air, when the cattle on your hills, when the fish of the sea, and the reptiles that crawl, shall be unable to distinguish the slave from a brute, then I will argue with you that the slave is a man!

For the present it is enough to affirm the equal manhood of the Negro race. Is it not astonishing that, while we are plowing, planting, and reaping, using all kinds of mechanical tools, erecting houses, constructing bridges, building ships, working in metals of brass, iron, copper, silver, and gold; that while we are reading, writing, and ciphering, acting as clerks, merchants, and secretaries, having among us lawyers, doctors, ministers, poets, authors, editors, orators, and teachers; that we are engaged in all the enterprises common to other men—digging gold in California, capturing the whale in the Pacific, feeding sheep and cattle on the hillside, living, moving, acting, thinking, planning, living in families as husbands, wives, and children, and above all, confessing and worshipping the Christian God, and looking hopefully for life and immortality beyond the grave—we are called upon to prove that we are men?

Freedom Is a Natural Right

Would you have me argue that man is entitled to liberty? That he is the rightful owner of his own body? You have already declared it. Must I argue the wrongfulness of slavery? Is that a question for republicans? Is it to be settled by the rules of logic and argumentation, as a matter beset with great difficulty, involving a doubtful application of the principle of justice, hard to understand? How should I look today in the presence of Americans, dividing and subdividing a discourse, to show that men have a natural right to freedom, speaking of it relatively and positively, negatively and affirmatively? To do so would be to make myself ridiculous, and to offer an insult to your understanding. There is not a man beneath the canopy of heaven who does not know that slavery is wrong for him.

What! Am I to argue that it is wrong to make men brutes, to rob them of their liberty, to work them without wages, to keep them ignorant of their relations to their fellow men, to beat them with sticks, to flay their flesh with the lash, to load their limbs with irons, to hunt them with dogs, to sell them at auction, to sunder their families, to knock out their teeth, to burn their flesh, to starve them into obedience and submission to their masters? Must I argue that a system thus marked with blood and stained with pollution is wrong? No—I will not. I have better employment for my time and strength than such arguments would imply.

What, then, remains to be argued? Is it that slavery is not divine; that God did not establish it; that our doctors of divinity are mistaken? There is blasphemy in the thought. That which is inhuman cannot be divine. Who can reason on such a proposition? They that can, may—I cannot. The time for such argument is past.

America's Crimes Against God and Men

At a time like this, scorching irony, not convincing argument, is needed. Oh! had I the ability, and could I reach the nation's ear, I would today pour out a fiery stream of biting ridicule, blasting reproach, withering sarcasm, and stern rebuke. For it is not light that is needed, but fire; it is not the gentle shower, but thunder. We need the storm, the whirlwind, and the earthquake. The feeling of the nation must be quickened; the conscience of the nation must be roused; the propriety of the nation must be startled; the hypocrisy of the nation must be exposed; and its crimes against God and man must be denounced.

What to the American slave is your Fourth of July? I answer, a day that reveals to him more than all other days of the year, the gross injustice and cruelty to which he is the constant victim. To him your celebration is a sham; your boasted liberty an unholy license; your national greatness, swelling vanity; your sounds of rejoicing are empty and heartless; your shouts of liberty and equality, hollow mock; your prayers and hymns, your sermons and thanksgivings, with all your religious parade and solemnity, are to him mere bombast, fraud, deception, impiety, and hypocrisy—a thin veil to cover up crimes which would disgrace a nation of savages. There is not a nation of the earth guilty of practices more shocking and bloody than are the people of these United States at this very hour.

Go search where you will, roam through all the monarchies and despotisms of the Old World, travel through South America, search out every abuse and when you have found the last, lay your facts by the side of the everyday practices of this nation, and you will say with me that, for revolting barbarity and shameless hypocrisy, America reigns without a rival.

What the Black Man Wants

Frederick Douglass

Throughout the Civil War, Frederick Douglass remained a tireless advocate of black civil rights, among the first to demand that blacks be allowed to serve in the Union army and he often clashed with Abraham Lincoln's cautious policies. In early 1865 a Union victory was at last in sight, and with it, the permanent eradication of slavery. However, Douglass believed there was still much work to be done on behalf of the embattled former slaves. The following selection, a speech that Douglass addressed to the Massachusetts Anti-Slavery Society only days before the war's end and Lincoln's subsequent assassination, focuses on the importance of securing for blacks legal equality. Douglass argues that freedom alone is insufficient unless accompanied by the full rights of citizenship, particularly the right to vote. He recognizes that the defeat of the Confederacy will not end southern hostility, prejudice, and resentment. He mocks the charge leveled by many whites in the North as well as in the South that blacks are too ignorant to vote. Douglass reminds his audience that granting blacks the right to vote is not only morally right but also a matter of honor and patriotism.

❧ ❧ ❧

Frederick Douglass, address to the Annual Meeting of the Massachusetts Anti-Slavery Society, Boston, MA, April 1865.

I came here, as I come always to the meetings in New England, as a listener, and not as a speaker; and one of the reasons why I have not been more frequently to the meetings of this society, has been because of the disposition on the part of some of my friends to call me out upon the platform, even when they knew that there was some difference of opinion and of feeling between those who rightfully belong to this platform and myself; and for fear of being misconstrued, as desiring to interrupt or disturb the proceedings of these meetings, I have usually kept away, and have thus been deprived of that educating influence, which I am always free to confess is of the highest order, descending from this platform. I have felt, since I have lived out West [Douglass means west of Boston, in Rochester, NY], that in going there I parted from a great deal that was valuable; and I feel, every time I come to these meetings, that I have lost a great deal by making my home west of Boston, west of Massachusetts; for, if anywhere in the country there is to be found the highest sense of justice, or the truest demands for my race, I look for it in the East, I look for it here. The ablest discussions of the whole question of our rights occur here, and to be deprived of the privilege of listening to those discussions is a great deprivation.

I do not know, from what has been said, that there is any difference of opinion as to the duty of abolitionists, at the present moment. How can we get up any difference at this point, or any point, where we are so united, so agreed? I went especially, however, with that word of Mr [Wendell] Phillips [a prominent abolitionist], which is the criticism of Gen. [Nathaniel P.] Banks and Gen. Banks' policy. [Gen. Banks instituted a labor policy in Louisiana that was discriminatory of blacks, claiming that it was to help prepare them to better handle freedom. Wendell Phillips countered by saying, "If there is anything patent in the whole history of our thirty years' struggle, it is that the Negro no more needs to be prepared for liberty than the white man."] I hold that that policy is our chief danger at the present moment; that it practically enslaves the Negro, and makes the Proclamation [the Emancipation Proclamation] of 1863 a mockery and delusion. What is freedom? It is the right to choose one's own employment. Certainly it means that, if it means anything; and when any individual or combination of individuals undertakes to decide for any man when he shall work, where he shall work, at what he shall work, and for what he shall work, he or they practically reduce him to slavery. [Applause.] He is a slave. That I understand Gen. Banks to do—to determine for the so-called freedman, when, and where, and at what, and for how much he shall work, when he shall be punished, and by whom punished. It is absolute slavery. It defeats the beneficent intention of the Government, if it has beneficent intentions, in regards to the freedom of our people.

I have had but one idea for the last three years to present to the American people, and the phraseology in which I clothe it is the old abolition phraseology. I am for the "immediate, unconditional, and universal" enfranchisement of the black man, in every State in the Union. [Loud applause.] Without this, his liberty is a mockery; without this, you might as well almost retain the old name of slavery for his condition; for in fact, if he is not the slave of the individual master, he is the slave of society, and holds his liberty as a privilege, not as a right. He is at the mercy of the mob, and has no means of protecting himself.

It may be objected, however, that this pressing of the Negro's right to suffrage is premature. Let us have slavery abolished, it may be said, let us have labor organized, and then, in the natural course of events, the right of suffrage will be extended to the Negro. I do not agree with this. The constitution of the human mind is such, that if it once disregards the conviction forced upon it by a revelation of truth, it requires the exercise of a higher power to produce the same conviction afterwards. The American people are now in tears. The Shenandoah has run blood—the best blood of the North. All around Richmond, the blood of New England and of the North has been shed—of your sons, your brothers and your fathers. We all feel, in the existence of this Rebellion, that judgments terrible, widespread, far-reaching, overwhelming, are abroad in the land; and we feel, in view of these judgments, just now, a disposition to learn righteousness. This is the hour. Our streets are in mourning, tears are falling at every fireside, and under the chastisement of this Rebellion we have almost come up to the point of conceding this great, this all-important right of suffrage. I fear that if we fail to do it now, if abolitionists fail to press it now, we may not see, for centuries to come, the same disposition that exists at this moment. [Applause.] Hence, I say, now is the time to press this right.

Why the Black Man Needs Suffrage

It may be asked, "Why do you want it? Some men have got along very well without it. Women have not this right." Shall we justify one wrong by another? This is the sufficient answer. Shall we at this moment justify the deprivation of the Negro of the right to vote, because some one else is deprived of that privilege? I hold that women, as well as men, have the right to vote [applause], and my heart and voice go with the movement to extend suffrage to woman; but that question rests upon another basis than which our right rests. We may be asked, I say, why we want it. I will tell you why we want it. We want it because it is our right, first of all. No class of men can, without insulting their own nature, be content with any deprivation of their rights. We want it again, as a means for educating our race. Men are so constituted that they derive their conviction of their own possibilities largely by the estimate formed of them by others. If nothing is expected of a people, that people will find it difficult to contradict that expectation. By depriving us of suffrage, you affirm our incapacity to form an intelligent judgment respecting public men and public measures; you declare before the world that we are unfit to exercise the elective franchise, and by this means lead us to undervalue ourselves, to put a low estimate upon ourselves, and to feel that we have no possibilities like other men. Again, I want the elective franchise, for one, as a colored man, because ours is a peculiar government, based upon a peculiar idea, and that idea is universal suffrage. If I were in a monarchial government, or an autocratic or aristocratic government, where the few bore rule and the many were subject, there would be no special stigma resting upon me, because I did not exercise the elective franchise. It would do me no great violence. Mingling with the mass I should partake of the strength of the mass; I should be supported by the mass, and I should have the same incentives to endeavor with the mass of my fellow-men; it would be no particular burden, no particular deprivation; but here where universal suffrage is the rule, where that is the fundamental idea of the Government, to rule us out is to make us an exception, to brand us with the stigma of inferiority, and to invite to our heads the missiles of those about us; therefore, I want the franchise for the black man.

There are, however, other reasons, not derived from any consideration merely of our rights, but arising out of the conditions of the South, and of the country—

considerations which have already been referred to by
Mr. Phillips—considerations which must arrest the attention of statesmen. I believe that when the tall heads
of this Rebellion shall have been swept down, as they
will be swept down, when the [Jefferson] Davises and
[Robert] Toombses and [Alexander] Stephenses, and
others who are leading this Rebellion shall have been
blotted out, there will be this rank undergrowth of treason, to which reference has been made, growing up
there, and interfering with, and thwarting the quiet operation of the Federal Government in those states. You
will see those traitors, handing down, from sire to son,
the same malignant spirit which they have manifested
and which they are now exhibiting, with malicious
hearts, broad blades, and bloody hands in the field,
against our sons and brothers. That spirit will still remain; and whoever sees the Federal Government extended over those Southern States will see that Government in a strange land, and not only in a strange
land, but in an enemy's land. A post-master of the
United States in the South will find himself surrounded
by a hostile spirit; a collector in a Southern port will
find himself surrounded by a hostile spirit; a United
States marshal or United States judge will be surrounded there by a hostile element. That enmity will
not die out in a year, will not die out in an age. The
Federal Government will be looked upon in those
States precisely as the Governments of Austria and
France are looked upon in Italy at the present moment.
They will endeavor to circumvent, they will endeavor
to destroy, the peaceful operation of this Government.
Now, where will you find the strength to counterbal-
ance this spirit, if you do not find it in the Negroes of
the South? They are your friends, and have always been
your friends. They were your friends even when the
Government did not regard them as such. They com-

prehended the genius of this war before you did. It is a significant fact, it is a marvellous fact, it seems almost to imply a direct interposition of Providence, that this war, which began in the interest of slavery on both sides, bids fair to end in the interest of liberty on both sides. [Applause.] It was begun, I say, in the interest of slavery on both sides. The South was fighting to take slavery out of the Union, and the North was fighting to keep it in the Union; the South fighting to get it beyond the limits of the United States Constitution, and the North fighting to retain it within those limits; the South fighting for new guarantees, and the North fighting for the old guarantees;— both despising the Negro, both insulting the Negro. Yet, the Negro, apparently endowed with wisdom from on high, saw more clearly the end from the beginning than we did. When [Secretary of State William H.] Seward said the status of no man in

Frederick Douglass

the country would be changed by the war, the Negro did not believe him. [Applause.] When our generals sent their underlings in shoulder-straps to hunt the flying Negro back from our lines into the jaws of slavery, from which he had escaped, the Negroes thought that a mistake had been made, and that the intentions of the Government had not been rightly understood by our officers in shoulder-straps, and they continued to come into our lines, threading their way through bogs and fens, over briers and thorns, fording streams, swimming rivers, bringing us tidings as to the safe path to march, and pointing out the dangers that threatened us.

They are our only friends in the South, and we should be true to them in this their trial hour, and see to it that they have the elective franchise.

The Charge of "Inferiority"

I know that we are inferior to you in some things—virtually inferior. We walk about you like dwarfs among giants. Our heads are scarcely seen above the great sea of humanity. The Germans are superior to us; the Irish are superior to us; the Yankees are superior to us [Laughter]; they can do what we cannot, that is, what we have not hitherto been allowed to do. But while I make this admission, I utterly deny, that we are originally, or naturally, or practically, or in any way, or in any important sense, inferior to anybody on this globe. [Loud applause.] This charge of inferiority is an old dodge. It has been made available for oppression on many occasions. It is only about six centuries since the blue-eyed and fair-haired Anglo-Saxons were considered inferior by the haughty Normans, who once trampled upon them. If you read the history of the Norman Conquest, you will find that this proud Anglo-Saxon was once looked upon as of coarser clay than his Norman master, and might be found in the highways and byways of Old England laboring with a brass collar on his neck, and the name of his master marked upon it. You were down then! [Laughter and applause.] You are up now. I am glad you are up, and I want you to be glad to help us up also. [Applause.]

The story of our inferiority is an old dodge, as I have said; for wherever men oppress their fellows, wherever they enslave them, they will endeavor to find the needed apology for such enslavement and oppression in the character of the people oppressed and enslaved. When we wanted, a few years ago, a slice of Mexico, it was hinted that the Mexicans were an inferior race, that the old Castilian blood had become so weak that it would scarcely run down hill, and that Mexico needed the long, strong and beneficent arm of the Anglo-Saxon care extended over it. We said that it was necessary to its salvation, and a part of the "manifest destiny" of this Republic, to extend our arm over that dilapidated government. So, too, when Russia wanted to take possession of a part of the Ottoman Empire, the Turks were an "inferior race." So, too, when England wants to set the heel of her power more firmly in the quivering heart of old Ireland, the Celts are an "inferior race." So, too, the Negro, when he is to be robbed of any right which is justly his, is an "inferior man." It is said that we are ignorant; I admit it. But if we know enough to be hung, we know enough to vote. If the Negro knows enough to pay taxes to support the government, he knows enough to vote; taxation and representation should go together. If he knows enough to shoulder a musket and fight for the flag, fight for the government, he knows enough to vote. If he knows as much when he is sober as an Irishman knows when drunk, he knows enough to vote, on good American principles. [Laughter and applause.]

A Sense of Honor

But I was saying that you needed a counterpoise in the persons of the slaves to the enmity that would exist at the South after the Rebellion is put down. I hold that the American people are bound, not only in self-defence, to extend this right to the freedmen of the South, but they are bound by their love of country, and by all their regard for the future safety of those Southern States, to do this —to do it as a measure essential to the preservation of peace there. But I will not dwell upon this. I put it to the American sense of honor. The honor of a nation is an important thing. It is said in the Scriptures, "What doth it profit a man if he gain the whole world, and lose his own soul?" It may be said, also, What doth it profit a nation if it gain the whole world, but lose its honor? I hold that the American government has taken upon itself solemn obligation of honor, to see that this war—let it be long or short, let it cost much or let it cost little—that this war shall not cease until every freedman at the South has the right to vote. [Applause.] It has bound itself to it. What have you asked the black men of the South, the black men of the whole country to do? Why, you have asked them to incure the enmity of their masters, in order to befriend you and to befriend this Government. You have asked us to call down, not only upon ourselves, but upon our children's children, the deadly hate of the entire Southern people. You have called upon us to turn our backs upon our masters, to abandon their cause and espouse yours; to turn against the South and in favor of the North; to shoot down the Confederacy and uphold the flag—the American flag. You have called upon us to expose ourselves to all the subtle machinations of their malignity for all time. And now, what do you propose to do when you come to make peace? To reward your enemies, and trample in the dust your friends? Do you intend to sacrifice the very men who have come to the rescue of your banner in the South, and incurred the lasting displeasure of their masters thereby? Do you intend to sacrifice them and reward your enemies? Do you mean to give your enemies the right to vote, and take it away from your friends? Is that wise policy? Is that honorable? Could American honor withstand such a blow? I do not believe you will do it. I think you will see to it that we have the right to vote. There is something too mean in looking upon the Negro, when you are in trouble, as a citizen, and when you are free from trouble, as an alien. When this nation was in trouble, in its early struggles, it looked upon the Negro as a citizen. In 1776 he was a citizen. At the time of the formation of the Consitution the

Negro had the right to vote in eleven States out of the old thirteen. In your trouble you have made us citizens. In 1812 Gen. [Andrew] Jackson addressed us as citizens— "fellow-citizens." He wanted us to fight. We were citizens then! And now, when you come to frame a conscription bill, the Negro is a citizen again. He has been a citizen just three times in the history of this government, and it has always been in time of trouble. In time of trouble we are citizens. Shall we be citizens in war, and aliens in peace? Would that be just?

Elevation Must Follow Freedom

I ask my friends who are apologizing for not insisting upon this right, where can the black man look, in this country, for the assertion of his right, if he may not look to the Massachusetts Anti-Slavery Society? Where under the whole heavens can he look for sympathy, in asserting this right, if he may not look to this platform? Have you lifted us up to a certain height to see that we are men, and then are any disposed to leave us there, without seeing that we are put in possession of all our rights? We look naturally to this platform for the assertion of all our rights, and for this one especially. I understand the anti-slavery societies of this country to be based on two principles,—first, the freedom of the blacks of this country; and, second, the elevation of them. Let me not be misunderstood here. I am not asking for sympathy at the hands of abolitionists, sympathy at the hands of any. I think the American people are disposed often to be generous rather than just. I look over this country at the present time, and I see Educational Societies, Sanitary Commissions, Freedmen's Associations, and the like,—all very good: but in regard to the colored people there is always more that is benevolent, I perceive, than just, manifested towards us. What I ask for the Negro is not benevolence, not pity, not sympathy, but simply justice. [Applause.] The American people have always been anxious to know what they shall do with us. Gen. Banks was distressed with solicitude as to what he should do with the Negro. Everybody has asked the question, and they learned to ask it early of the abolitionists, "What shall we do with the Negro?" I have had but one answer from the beginning. Do nothing with us! Your doing with us has already played the mischief with us. Do nothing with us! If the apples will not remain on the tree of their own strength, if they are wormeaten at the core, if they are early ripe and disposed to fall, let them fall! I am not for tying or fastening them on the tree in any way, except by nature's plan, and if they will not stay there, let them fall. And if the Negro cannot stand on his own legs, let him fall also. All I ask is, give him a chance to stand on his own legs! Let him alone! If you see him on his way to school, let him alone, don't disturb him! If you see him going to the dinner table at a hotel, let him go! If you see him going to the ballot-box, let him alone, don't disturb him! [Applause.] If you see him going into a work-shop, just let him alone,—your interference is doing him a positive injury. Gen. Banks' "preparation" is of a piece with this attempt to prop up the Negro. Let him fall if he cannot stand alone! If the Negro cannot live by the line of eternal justice, so beautifully pictured to you in the illustration used by Mr. Phillips, the fault will not be yours, it will be his who made the Negro, and established that line for his government. [Applause.] Let him live or die by that. If you will only untie his hands, and give him a chance, I think he will live. He will work as readily for himself as the white man. A great many delusions have been swept away by this war. One was, that the Negro would not work; he has proved his ability to work. Another was, that the Negro would not fight; that he possessed only the most sheepish attributes of humanity;

was a perfect lamb, or an "Uncle Tom;" disposed to take off his coat whenever required, fold his hands, and be whipped by anybody who wanted to whip him. But the war has proved that there is a great deal of human nature in the Negro, and that "he will fight," as Mr. Quincy [John Quincy Adams], our President, said, in earlier days than these, "when there is reasonable probability of his whipping anybody." [Laughter and applause.]

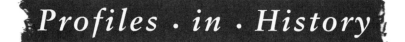

Profiles · in · History

Harriet Tubman: Heroine of the Underground Railroad

Harriet Tubman

Nancy A. Davidson

Harriet Tubman is best known as the fearless Underground Railroad "conductor" who led more than three hundred runaways to freedom. Born a slave in Dorchester County, Maryland, she grew up to become a leading abolitionist, suffragist, and friend to Frederick Douglass and John Brown. Although Tubman never learned to read or write, it is certain that she contributed as much to the cause of freedom as her more learned contemporaries, such as Douglass, Maria Stewart, and William Wells Brown. Her name has become virtually synonymous with the Underground Railroad; she remains to this day an enduring symbol of courage, determination, and commitment to universal freedom. The following selection, by author Nancy A. Davidson, provides a detailed portrait of the life behind the legend, commenting on Tubman's personal life, her affiliations with other abolitionists, and activism in the women's movement, aspects that complemented her role as the "Moses" of the Underground Railroad.

🐝 🐝 🐝

"I had crossed the line of which I had so long been dreaming. I was free; but there was no one to welcome

Nancy A. Davidson, "Harriet Tubman 'Moses,' (c. 1820 1913): Underground Railroad Conductor, Union Scout and Spy, Nurse, Feminist," *Notable Black American Women*, edited by Jessie Carney Smith. Farmington Hills, MI: Gale Research, Inc., 1992. Copyright © 1992 by Gale Research, Inc. Reproduced by permission.

me to the land of freedom," Harriet Tubman spoke of her accomplishment and the intense loneliness that led to her resolve to free her family and other slaves. Although she escaped from slavery, her heart was "down in the old cabin quarters, with the old folks and my brothers and sisters." With this resolve she began her work as a conductor on the Underground Railway, a venture that would last for ten years and make her famous. Tubman made at least fifteen trips from the North into southern slave states, leading over two hundred slaves into free northern states. On her first trip into slave territory, she led her sister, Mary Ann Bowley, and two children to freedom in the North, eventually freeing all her brothers and sisters as well as her parents. Although Harriet Tubman achieved historical importance primarily in this role, she was also a spy, nurse, feminist, and social reformer, if indeed these terms can adequately describe her various activities during a period of profound racial, social, and economic upheaval in the United States in the nineteenth century.

The term conductor was, of course, a euphemism for guide or leader, as the Underground Railroad was for illegal transportation. These terms have a romantic ring today, but Tubman's work was far from romantic; it was extremely dangerous and demanded great strength and endurance, both physically and mentally. Tubman's physical appearance was decidedly not that of a leader, as she was not an imposing figure like Sojourner Truth, a slave who became a famous orator and feminist. She was of slight build and only five feet tall. Even more curious for a person whose leadership depended upon physical action, Tubman suffered from seizures of sudden and deep sleep because of a head injury received as a young girl. Nevertheless, Tubman possessed leadership qualities that were quickly recognized by the slaves she led to freedom and the abolitionists with whom she worked. Thomas Wentworth Higginson, the author and reformer, called her "the greatest heroine of the age," in an 1859 letter to his mother. "Her tales of adventure are beyond anything in fiction and her ingenuity and generalship are extraordinary. I have known her for some time—the slaves call her Moses."

Small Stature, Great Courage

Tubman made up for her small size through the expedient of carrying a long rifle—a weapon she would use to encourage any slaves who became fainthearted during their journey north as well as to discourage proslavers—and her innate leadership abilities. She was not taught to read or write but relied upon her memory, knowledge of nature—the only resource she had at times when guiding slaves under cover of darkness—and natural shrewdness. When some whites expressed unusual curiosity while observing Tubman and some slaves in a small southern town, she bought railway tickets for a train going south. What slave attempting to escape from a southern state would travel south? The ploy was one of a number Tubman would use to elude escape from authorities. Tubman was well versed in the Bible, music, and folklore of her time and place in the South, and her repertoire of biblical verse and song was important in communicating. Harriet Tubman used her strong singing voice to communicate her presence to slaves in the South and to communicate danger or safety to slaves that were hidden while she was scouting their surroundings.

Tubman's unwavering resolve and courage, like that of other great leaders, is more difficult to account for. Scholars and historians can only examine the particular environment and events that produce leaders in particular places at particular times and speculate at the synergy of people, environment, and events. Of her environment, Tubman said, "I grew up like a neglected weed—ignorant of liberty, having no experience of it," when she was interviewed by Benjamin Drew, an educator and part-time journalist, in St. Catherines, Ontario, in the summer of 1855. Although she was ignorant of liberty as a slave. Tubman was nurtured and cared for in a large family. Born in 1820 in Dorchester County near Cambridge, Maryland, one of eleven children of Benjamin and Harriet (Green) Ross, Tubman was called Araminta as a child but later adopted the name of her mother. Tubman had stability of place while growing up, unlike some slaves who were sold to landowners in the deep South, although that stability was constantly under threat. Tubman was hired out for housework for families living near her owner at various times as a young child but was always returned to her family between jobs. While she and her family were subject to the orders of their owner and hired out to neighboring farmers, they were a family unit in which care and support was given and received and in which religion and folklore were shared.

The Effects of Slavery
Tubman was returned to the care of her family after a severe head injury, an injury that caused recurring seizures of sleep for the rest of her life. The injury had a profound influence on her emotionally as well as physically. When she was about thirteen years of age and working in the field one autumn, one of her fellow slaves left his field work early and went to the general store. The overseer caught up with the man in the store and attempted to bind him for a whipping. As the slave ran out the door, Tubman attempted to shield the man and was knocked unconscious by a two-pound weight the angry overseer had thrown at the running slave. She

recovered from the blow, but her convalescence was slow because the injury to her head was serious. While her body was healing, Tubman, raised in a deeply religious family, began praying. While seeking a solution to her condition as a slave, she began to examine that condition and, as well, the institution of slavery in general from a philosophical and practical perspective.

Speaking of this recovery period in her youth to her friend and biographer, Sarah Elizabeth Bradford, Tubman said "And so, as I lay so sick on my bed, from Christmas till March, I was always praying for poor old master. Oh, dear Lord, change that man's heart, and make him a Christian." Tubman's prayers changed when she heard that she and her brothers were to be sent in a chain gang to the far South. She prayed, "Lord, if you ain't never going to change that man's heart, kill him, Lord, and take him out of the way, so he won't do no more mischief." When her owner died shortly afterwards, Tubman again changed her prayers. She began praying in different ways and at different times for the Lord to "cleanse her heart of sin," beginning the process of taking control, so much as she could, of her life rather than passively accepting things as they were.

During this period of illness, prayer, and rumors of slave-selling, Tubman began to formulate a personal philosophy that transcended the laws of men. She trusted herself, God, and Divine Providence, in that order. Although she did not formulate this philosophy in a stroke of flashing illumination, it is probable that Tubman's character and intelligence, combined with the experience of her illness, prayer, and changing circumstances, produced an individual who, paradoxically, through both desire and necessity, developed self-reliant courage and strength of purpose. It was Tubman's courage and purpose that led her to become an important figure to both blacks and whites.

Recovery and Freedom

Tubman had a calm respite after she slowly healed from her injury. It was during this period that two events took place that are important: she married a free black man, and she discovered that her mother legally should have been freed years earlier upon the death of her former owner. Shortly after her recovery, her father became a valuable laborer for a neighboring timber operator, and Tubman began working for the man, slowly regaining her strength and becoming a valuable laborer also. In 1844, she married John Tubman, a free black in the Cambridge area. Little is known about Tubman's relationship with her husband; there are reports that he was not an ambitious man, and that he thought his wife worried too much about her condition as a slave. While Tubman was reticent about her relationship with John Tubman, she apparently cared for him. About a year after marrying, while she was still a slave, Tubman's curiosity about legal matters affecting the status of blacks led her to pay a lawyer to search for legal documents relating to her mother's owners to trace her mother's history in slavery. She discovered that her mother, Harriet Green Ross, had been legally free at one time because of the untimely death of one of her owners, a young woman named Mary Patterson who died young and unmarried, leaving no provisions for Harriet Green Ross. It was the lawyer's opinion that Tubman's mother was emancipated at that time. No one informed Harriet Ross of her rights, and she remained a slave. Although Tubman was illiterate, she examined the workings of literacy in a social order in which she had not power. Tubman realized that literacy had been denied her, but she began to understand the social order enslaved her. In 1849 Tubman escaped to freedom in Pennsylvania alone and unaided.

The self-reliance of Tubman was twofold: she began

supporting herself economically, and within a year of her escape, she began the task of freeing her relatives. Tubman's first stop was Baltimore, Maryland, for her sister and two children. Tubman embarked on her career as a conductor alone and unaided by the simple expedient of working as a cook and domestic in Philadelphia until she had saved enough money to provide for her needs. She provided for herself in between her trips to the South before the Civil War and also between her political interventions after the war.

Tubman Joins the Abolitionists

By 1857 she had freed her entire family, including her aging parents. John Bell Robinson, a pro-slavery advocate, criticized Tubman's work in his book *Pictures of Slavery and Freedom*, stating, "The most noted point in this act of horror was the bringing away from ease and comfortable homes two old slaves over seventy years of age." Pro-slavery writing criticizing Tubman was indicative not only of the economic damage she was responsible for in the South but also intended as a corrective to the increasing agitation in the North to abolish slavery. Tubman did not remember a life of ease and comfort as a slave. While Tubman began the work of leading her family and others from slavery to freedom in the North single-handedly after her own escape, she soon worked in concert with other abolitionists in the North, both black and white. The end of slavery was a personal issue for Harriet Tubman.

Tubman's self-appointed purpose led her to be closely involved with progressive social leaders in the North, first abolitionists, then feminists, and political and military leaders as she became well known as an abolitionist and a black leader. Her primary goal was to work for the freedom of slaves. Tubman's career led her to associate with people who shared her goal of the emancipation of blacks, regardless of the boundaries of gender, color, and socioeconomic status. She became closely associated with John Brown before his raid on the federal arsenal at Harper's Ferry and admired him enormously all of her life. Other white leaders she personally knew were Thomas Garrett and William H. Seward, as well as Susan B. Anthony, Ralph Waldo Emerson, and the Alcotts. The settlement and growth of the western states led to increased agitation over the institution of slavery, and white progressive leaders supported Tubman's work financially and welcomed her into their homes when she needed shelter, generally in conjunction with her trips to the South or when she was attending an antislavery feminist meeting. As the controversy over slavery intensified, Tubman became an effective and acknowledged leader in the abolitionist movement, which had a strong and effective organization in Philadelphia.

Organizing the Underground Railroad

As Boston was the center of progressive thought in New England, so Philadelphia was the center of progressive social thought and action further south on the Atlantic seaboard. It was in Philadelphia that Tubman became acquainted with William Still and other well-known and well-organized abolitionists. The first organized society against slavery was established in Philadelphia in 1775, the Pennsylvania Society for Promoting the Abolition of Slavery, the Relief of Free Negroes Unlawfully Held in Bondage, and for Improving the Condition of the African Race, indicating the long-held sympathetic views of the inhabitants. Tubman became closely associated with William Still, the energetic and active executive director of the General Vigilance Committee. Still was the most important black man that Tubman was closely associated with. The Underground Railroad

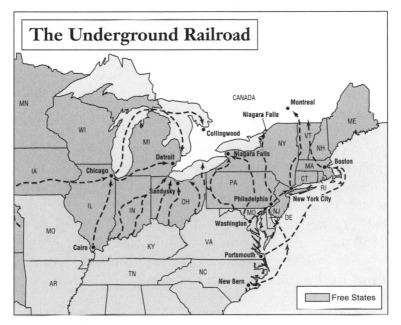

The Underground Railroad

was effectively organized into networks for the safe transport of slaves, and communication between leaders and workers in the system was necessary for safety and efficiency. On the other hand, written records were dangerous to keep, as abolitionists became aware after John Brown's papers were seized after the Harper's Ferry raid. Although many written records and letters were destroyed, Still kept a chronicle that has survived. Of Harriet Tubman he later wrote. "She was a woman of no pretensions; indeed, a more ordinary specimen of humanity could hardly be found among the most unfortunate-looking farm hands of the South. Yet in point of courage, shrewdness, and disinterested exertions to rescue her fellowman, she was without equal."

William Still and the other members of the General Vigilance Committee worked closely with Harriet Tubman; through their organization she met Thomas Garrett, a prominent white Quaker abolitionist in Wilmington, Delaware. Thomas Garrett thought highly of

Tubman and her work and provided her with shelter, money, or whatever else she needed for her trips on the Underground Railway, especially when Tubman was leading groups of slaves into Canada. He corresponded with friends united in the abolitionist movement as far away as Scotland, describing the activities of antislavers in the United States as well as Tubman's activities and raising money for her needs. His help was especially important as she freed members of her family from Delaware and began taking slaves to St. Catherines in western Canada for complete safety "under the lion's paw" of England. Passage of the Fugitive Slave Law in 1850 made freedom precarious for blacks in the North.

After living intermittently in St. Catherines, Ontario, from 1851 until 1857, Tubman moved to Auburn, New York, eventually settling there with her parents after the Civil War. Auburn was the center of progressive thought in New York. Abolition and women's suffrage thrived in Auburn. As well, it was the home of one of Harriet Tubman's strongest supporters, William H. Seward, [later] governor of New York, and a publishing center for abolitionist literature. William H. Seward sold Tubman a home in Auburn on generous terms, for which she paid through unsolicited donations from white supporters. At the annual meeting of the Massachusetts Anti-Slavery Society in 1859, the president, Thomas Wentworth Higginson, asked for a collection to assist her in buying the house so "her father and mother could support themselves, and enable her to resume the practice of her profession!" There was much "laughter and applause" after Higginson's announcement.

War and Reconstruction

Tubman's profession changed but little during the Civil War. She was sent to Beaufort after the fall of Port Royal, South Carolina, in 1862 for Reconstruction work by Governor Andrew of Massachusetts. Her position with the War Department was one of irregular attachment yet solicited by officials. Tubman nursed the sick and wounded soldiers and taught newly-freed blacks strategies for self-sufficiency. She was sent to Florida for a time to nurse soldiers who were ill with fever. After her return to South Carolina, she resumed her nursing duties there. When the young schoolteacher, Charlotte L. Forten, visited Beaufort, she enthusiastically wrote the following entry in her diary on 31 January 1863: "We spent all our time at Harriet Tubman's. She is a wonderful woman—a real heroine." Harriet Tubman also organized a group of eight black men to scout the inland waterway area of South Carolina for Union raids under the direction of Colonel James Montgomery. She personally assisted Colonel Montgomery when he led a raid in the Combahee area, coming under fire herself from Confederate troops in the battle.

Returning to Auburn after the Civil War, Tubman devoted herself to caring for her parents, raising funds for schools for former slaves, collecting clothes for destitute children, and helping the poor and disabled. Tubman worked closely with black churches that had provided overnight shelter for runaway slaves on the Underground Railroad and raised money for Tubman's work as a conductor. She was active in the growth of the AME [African Methodist Episcopal] Zion church in central and western New York and raised funds for the Thompson Memorial African Methodist Episcopal Zion [AMEZ] Church in Auburn. Always concerned with the most vulnerable—children and the elderly— Tubman was the agent of her church in collecting clothes for destitute children and was concerned with homes for the elderly. With her characteristic penchant for action, Tubman purchased twenty-five acres of land adjoining her house in 1896. The land was to be sold at auction, and Tubman hid in a corner of the crowd, bidding on the property until all others dropped out. It was not until she won the bidding that she identified herself as the buyer. The astonished crowd wondered where she would obtain the money for her purchase, but Harriet Tubman went to the bank and secured funds by mortgage. The Harriet Tubman Home for Aged and Indigent Colored People was incorporated in 1903 with the assistance of the AMEZ church, and formally opened in 1908.

Tubman resumed her affiliation with women's groups because she viewed racial liberation and women's liberation as being strongly linked. Tubman had a long-lasting and cordial relationship with the suffragist pioneer and leader, Susan B. Anthony, both being active in the New England Anti-Slavery Society. Tubman strongly believed in racial equality and thought that the greatest benefit could be reaped when blacks and whites worked together. She was also a delegate to the first annual convention of the National Federation of Afro-American Women in 1896 and when she was asked to give a talk at this first meeting, her theme was "More Homes for Our Aged." Victoria Earle Matthews, chairperson of the evening session, introduced Mother Harriet, as she was called, and commented on the great services that she had rendered to the race. Tubman's initial appearance before the delegates as speaker was a momentous occasion:

> Mrs. Tubman stood alone on the front of the rostrum, the audience, which not only filled every seat, but also much of the standing room in the aisles, rose as one person and greeted her with the waving of handerchiefs and clapping of hands. This was kept up for at least one minute, and Mrs. Tubman was much affected by the hearty reception given her.

The National Association of Colored Women would later pay for Tubman's funeral and for the marble headstone over her grave. In April 1897 the New England Women's Suffrage Association held a reception in her honor. When asked later in life whether she believed that women should have the right to vote. Tubman replied, "I have suffered enough to believe it."

Tubman Remarries

While Tubman was active in Reconstruction work, women's rights organizations, and in caring for her parents in her home, she also remarried. Her first husband, John Tubman, did not join her after her dash for freedom, and he died in 1867. In 1869 Tubman married a Union soldier, Nelson Davis, a black man twenty-two years younger than she. Little is known of Davis except that he was a former slave who served in the Union Army. The facts that have survived him are a result of documentation of his war service, documentation that enabled Harriet Tubman to draw a pension after his death as the widow of a Civil War veteran. For two decades white supporters attempted unsuccessfully to secure a government pension for Tubman based upon her three years of service during the Civil War. The only other facts about the marriage of Tubman to Nelson Davis come from a description of the wedding ceremony that appeared in an unidentified Auburn newspaper. Earl Conrad, in his book, *Harriet Tubman*, states, "It has been said that her husband, Nelson Davis, in spite of being a large man was not a healthy man, that he suffered with tuberculosis, and she married him to take care of him." This information was based upon an oral statement of a friend. The fact that Nelson Davis lived for twenty years after his marriage to Tubman appears to invalidate this claim and to reflect Victorian patriarchal sentiments. Other writers assert that Tubman cared deeply for her first husband because she kept his name. Tubman probably did care for her first husband, but again, retaining the Tubman surname was probably a practical matter for Tubman because of her age and fame, rather than a mythic and romantic matter. Tubman's second marriage, a marriage to a much younger man, has consistently been marginalized even by scholars and writers today. Readers of biographies and articles on Tubman's life are required to pay close attention to dates of births and deaths to discover that Harriet Tubman was a vital woman in middle age—not just a very good nurse.

Tubman died of pneumonia on March 10, 1913, after a two-year residence in the Harriet Tubman Home for Aged and Indigent Colored People. A memorial service was held a year later by the citizens of Auburn, at which time a tablet erected in her honor was unveiled. Booker T. Washington was the featured speaker at the evening service. Although biographies of Tubman contain elements of myth as well as fact, her fame has endured, most recently because of new interest in the role of women in history and in literature. A liberty ship was christened the *Harriet Tubman* during World War II, and in 1978 the United States Postal Service issued a Harriet Tubman commemorative stamp, the first in a Black Heritage USA Series. Poets, artists, and musicians have written, portrayed, and sung their admiration of this nineteenth-century black woman. Harriet Tubman personified strength and the quest for freedom, and her fame is enduring.

The Most Remarkable Woman of This Age

Commonwealth

From its beginnings, the abolitionist movement employed the power of the press, especially pamphlets and newspapers, to spread its message. Proslavery southerners were so alarmed by the proliferation of abolitionist literature that they sought repeatedly to ban its distribution in the region and to enact laws to proscribe teaching slaves to read. Nonetheless, abolitionist newspapers flourished in the North throughout the Civil War; these included Benjamin Lundy's *Genius of Universal Emancipation*, Elijah Lovejoy's *Alton (Ohio) Observer* (whose antislavery stance resulted in Lovejoy's 1837 murder by a mob), and the two most famous papers, William Lloyd Garrison's *Liberator* and Frederick Douglass's *North Star*. Not only did the newspapers aspire to persuade others to join the antislavery cause, but they also celebrated the inspirational courage of the movement's leading figures, such as Harriet Tubman. The following selection is an 1863 tribute to Tubman that appeared in the antislavery journal the *Commonwealth*. Its date of publication, 1863, is significant because the operations of the Underground Railroad were carefully guarded secrets lest public disclosure betray escape plans and routes

"The Most Remarkable Woman of This Age," *Commonwealth*, July 17, 1863.

to slaveholders and bounty hunters. If the Civil War had made escape all the more dangerous, emancipation also voided the Fugitive Slave Law while the proximity of Union troops offered a nearby safe haven for runaways.

🐝   🐝   🐝

Harriet Tubman, the famous fugitive slave from Maryland, risks her life sneaking into slave territory to free slaves. Slaveholders posted a $40,000 reward for the capture of the "Black Moses."

One of the teachers lately commissioned by the New-England Freedmen's Aid Society is probably the most remarkable woman of this age. That is to say, she has performed more wonderful deeds by the native power of her own spirit against adverse circumstances than any other. She is well known to many by the various names which her eventful life has given her; Harriet Garrison, Gen. Tubman, &c.; but among the slaves she is universally known by her well earned title of Moses,—Moses the deliverer. She is a rare instance, in the midst of high civilization and intellectual culture, of a being of great native powers, working powerfully, and to beneficient ends, entirely untaught by schools or books.

Her Life as a Slave

Her maiden name was Araminta Ross. She is the grand-daughter of a native African, and has not a drop of white blood in her veins. She was born in 1820 or 1821, on the Eastern Shore of Maryland. . . .

She seldom lived with her owner, but was usually "hired out" to different persons. She once "hired her time," and employed it in the rudest farming labors, ploughing, carting, driving the oxen, &c., to so good advantage that she was able in one year to buy a pair of steers worth forty dollars.

When quite young she lived with a very pious mistress; but the slaveholder's religion did not prevent her from whipping the young girl for every slight or fancied fault. Araminta found that this was usually a morning exercise; so she prepared for it by putting on all the thick clothes she could procure to protect her skin. She made sufficient outcry, however, to convince her mistress that her blows had full effect; and in the afternoon she would take off her wrappings, and dress as well as she could. When invited into family prayers, she preferred to stay on the landing, and pray for herself; "and I prayed to God," she says "to make me strong and able to fight and that's what I've [always] prayed for ever since. . . ."

In her youth she received a severe blow on her head from a heavy weight thrown by her master at another slave, but which accidentally hit her. The blow produced a disease of the brain which was severe for a long time, and still makes her very lethargic. . . . She was married about 1844 to a free colored man named John Tubman, but never had any children. Owing to changes in her owner's family, it was determined to sell her and some other slaves; but her health was so much injured, that a purchaser was not easily found. At length she became convinced that she would soon be carried away, and she decided to escape. Her brothers did not agree with her plans, and she walked off alone, following the guidance of the brooks, which she had observed to run North. . . .

Harriet Becomes "Moses"

She remained two years in Philadelphia working hard and carefully hoarding her money. Then she hired a room, furnished it as well as she could, bought a nice suit of men's clothes, and went back to Maryland for her husband. But the faithless man had taken to himself another wife. Harriet did not dare venture into her presence, but sent word to her husband where she was. He declined joining her. At first her grief and anger were excessive . . . but finally she thought . . . "if he could do without her, she could without him," and so "he dropped out of her heart," and she determined to give her life to brave deeds. Thus all personal aims died out of her heart; and with her simple brave motto, "I can't die but once," she began the work which has made her Moses,— the deliverer of her people. Seven or eight times she has returned to the neighborhood of her former home, always at the risk of death in the most terrible forms, and each time has brought away a company of fugitive slaves, and led them safely to the free States, or to Canada. Every time she went, the dangers increased. In 1857, she brought away her old parents, and, as they were too feeble to walk, she was obliged to hire a wagon, which added greatly to the perils of the journey. In 1860 she went for the last time, and among her troop was an infant whom they were obliged to keep stupefied with laudanum to prevent its outcries. . . .

Secrecy and Danger

She always came in the winter when the nights are long and dark, and people who have homes stay in them. She was never seen on the plantation herself, but appointed a rendezvous for her company eight or ten miles distant; so that if they were discovered at the first start she was not compromised. She started on Saturday night; the slaves at that time being allowed to go away from home to visit their friends—so that they would not be missed until Monday morning. Even then they were supposed to have loitered on the way, and it would often be late on Monday afternoon before the flight would be certainly known. If by any further delay the advertisement was not sent out before Tuesday morning, she felt secure of keeping ahead of it; but if it were, it required all her ingenuity to escape. She resorted to various devices, she had confidential friends all along the road. She would hire a man to follow the one who put up the notices, and take them down as soon as his back was turned. She crossed creeks on railroad bridges by night, she hid her company in the woods while she herself not being advertised went into the towns in search of information. . . . The expedition was governed by the strictest rules. If any man gave out, he must be shot. "Would you really do that?" she was asked. "Yes," she replied, "if he was weak enough to give out, he'd be weak enough to betray us all, and all who had helped us; and do you think I'd let so many die just for one coward man." "Did you ever have to shoot any one?" she was asked. "One time," she said, "a man gave out on the second night; his feet were sore and swollen, he couldn't go any further; he'd rather go back and die, if he must." They tried all arguments in vain, bathed his feet, tried to strengthen him, but it was of no use, he would go back. Then she said, "I told the boys to get their guns ready, and shoot him. They'd have done it in a minute; but when he heard that, he jumped right up and went on as well as any body. . . ."

When going on these journeys she often lay alone in the forests all night. Her whole soul was filled with awe of the mysterious Unseen Presence, which thrilled her with such depths of emotion, that all other care and fear vanished. Then she seemed to speak with her Maker "as a man talketh with his friend;" her child-like petitions had direct answers, and beautiful visions lifted her up above all doubt and anxiety into serene trust and faith. No man can be a hero without this faith in some form; the sense that he walks not in his own strength, but leaning on an almighty arm. Call it fate, destiny, what you will, Moses of old, Moses of to-day, believed it to be Almighty God.

Harriet, the Moses of Her People

Sarah H. Bradford

The Fugitive Slave Law of 1850 raised the risks for blacks in free states as well as for those abetting them. Even black Americans who had either been granted emancipation or born into freedom were at jeopardy, as they were denied due process and a jury trial if charged with running away by a party claiming to be the slave's owner or by bounty hunters. The Fugitive Slave Law also criminalized helping or harboring escapees. As a result, Canada became more and more often the promised land for runaways, and northern states that shared Canadian borders (especially Vermont, New York, and Michigan) became important stops along the Underground Railroad.

The Fugitive Slave Law had another unintended consequence: It fostered northern sympathy for runaways and resentment that ordinary citizens could be legally punished for assisting them. The Anthony Burns incident in Boston in 1854 aroused the wrath of thousands of citizens, fifty thousand of whom took to the streets to protest the forced return of fugitive Burns. The incident also inspired Henry David Thoreau to write his celebrated abolitionist essay "Slavery in Massachusetts." The following selection, from abolitionist schoolteacher Sarah H. Bradford's biography of her friend Harriet Tubman, describes a similar incident of

Sarah H. Bradford, "Incident in Troy, New York," *Harriet, the Moses of Her People*. New York: G.R. Lockwood & Son, 1886.

civil disobedience in which citizens of Troy, New York, led by Tubman, rallied to the aid of a fugitive and prevented his capture. Bradford's account, although written during the 1880s, paints a vivid and immediate picture of Tubman's strength, courage, and imposing presence. The physical attributes of the runaway, who appeared to be "white," are also telling. Many slaves were of mixed race due to the frequency with which white masters used the black women as sexual chattels. But even if the slave's father had been his or her owner, he was still deemed "colored" under the law and was denied basic human rights.

❧   ❧   ❧

In the spring of 1860, Harriet Tubman was requested by Mr. Gerrit Smith [a prominent abolitionist] to go to Boston to attend a large Anti-Slavery meeting. On her way, she stopped at Troy to visit a cousin, and while there the colored people were one day startled with the intelligence that a fugitive slave, by the name of Charles Nalle, had been followed by his master (who was his younger brother, and not one grain whiter than he), and that he was already in the hands of the officers, and was to be taken back to the South. The instant Harriet heard the news, she started for the office of the United States Commissioner, scattering the tidings as she went. An excited crowd was gathered about the office, through which Harriet forced her way, and rushed up stairs to the door of the room where the fugitive was detained. A wagon was already waiting before the door to carry off the man, but the crowd was even then so great, and in such a state of excitement, that the officers did not dare to bring the man down. On the opposite side of the street stood the colored people, watching the window where they could see Harriet's sun-bonnet, and feeling assured that so long as she stood there, the fugitive was still in the office. Time passed on, and he did not appear. "They've taken him out another way, depend upon that," said some of the colored people. "No," replied others, "there stands Moses yet, and as long as she is there, he is safe." Harriet, now seeing the necessity for a tremendous effort for his rescue, sent out some little boys to cry fire.

Tubman Stands Her Ground
The bells rang, the crowd increased, till the whole street was a dense mass of people. Again and again the officers

Remembering Harriet Tubman

The following selection is an excerpt from a letter written by the Quaker abolitionist Thomas Garrett in which he reminisces about Tubman's heroic role in the Underground Railroad.

The date of the commencement of her labors, I cannot certainly give; but I think it must have been about 1845; from that time till 1860, I think she must have brought from the neighborhood where she had been held as a slave from 60 to 80 persons, from Maryland, some 80 miles from here.

No slave who placed himself under her care, was ever arrested that I have heard of; she mostly had her regular stopping places on her route; but in one instance, when she had several stout men with her, some 30 miles below here, she said that God told her to stop, which she did; and then asked him what she must do. He told her to leave the road, and turn to the left; she obeyed, and soon came to a small stream of tide water; there was no boat, no bridge; she again inquired of her Guide what she was to do. She was told to go through. It was cold, in the came out to try and clear the stairs, and make a way to take their captive down; others were driven down, but Harriet stood her ground, her head bent and her arms folded. "Come, old woman, you must get out of this," said one of the officers; "I must have the way, cleared; if you can't get down alone, some one will help you." Harriet, still putting on a greater appearance of decrepitude, twitched away from him, and kept her place. Offers were made to buy Charles from his master, who at first agreed to take twelve hundred dollars for him; but when this was subscribed, he immediately raised the price to fifteen hundred. The crowd grew more excited. A gen-

month of March; but having confidence in her Guide, she went in; the water came up to her armpits; the men refused to follow till they saw her safe on the opposite shore. They then followed, and, if I mistake not, she had soon to wade a second stream; soon after which she came to a cabin of colored people, who took them all in, put them to bed, and dried their clothes, ready to proceed next night on their journey. Harriet had run out of money, and gave them some of her underclothing to pay for their kindness.

When she called on me two days after, she was so hoarse she could hardly speak, and was also suffering with violent toothache. The strange part of the story we found to be, that the masters of these men had put up the previous day, at the railroad station near where she left, an advertisement for them, offering a large reward for their apprehension; but they made a safe exit. She at one time brought as many as seven or eight, several of whom were women and children. She was well known here in Chester County [Delaware] and Philadelphia, and re-spected by all true abolitionists.

Thomas Garrett, letter to Sarah H. Bradford, June 1866.

tleman raised a window and called out, "Two hundred dollars for his rescue, but not one cent to his master!" This was responded to by a roar of satisfaction from the crowd below. At length the officers appeared, and announced to the crowd, that if they would open a lane to the wagon, they would promise to bring the man down the front way. The lane was opened, and the man was brought out—a tall, handsome, intelligent white man, with his wrists manacled together, walking between the U.S. Marshal and another officer, and behind him his brother and his master, so like him that one could hardly be told from the other.

A Daring Rescue

The moment they appeared, Harriet roused from her stooping posture, threw up a window, and cried to her friends: "Here he comes—take him!" and then darted down the stairs like a wild-cat. She seized one officer and pulled him down, then another, and tore him away from the man; and keeping her arms about the slave, she cried to her friends: Drag us out! Drag him to the river! Drown him! but don't let them have him!" They were knocked down together, and while down, she tore off her sun-bonnet and tied it on the head of the fugitive. When he rose, only his head could be seen, and amid the surging mass of people the slave was no longer recognized, while the master appeared like the slave. Again and again they were knocked down, the poor slave utterly helpless, with his manacled wrists, streaming with blood. Harriet's outer clothes were torn from her, and even her stout shoes were pulled from her feet, yet she never relinquished her hold of the man, till she had dragged him to the river, where he was tumbled into a boat, Harriet following in a ferry-boat to the other side. But the telegraph was ahead of them, and as soon as they landed he was seized and hurried from her sight.

After a time, some school children came hurrying along, and to her anxious inquiries they answered, "He is up in that house, in the third story." Harriet rushed up to the place. Some men were attempting to make their way up the stairs. The officers were firing down, and two men were lying on the stairs, who had been shot. Over their bodies our heroine rushed, and with the help of others burst open the door of the room, and dragged out the fugitive, whom Harriet carried down stairs in her arms. A gentleman who was riding by with a fine horse, stopped to ask what the disturbance meant; and on hearing the story, his sympathies seemed to be thoroughly aroused; he sprang from his wagon, calling out, "That is a blood-horse, drive him till he drops." The poor man was hurried in; some of his friends jumped in after him, and drove at the most rapid rate to Schenectady.

CHAPTER

4

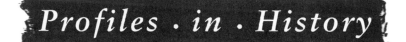

Profiles · in · History

Other
Groundbreakers

Who Was Nat Turner?

Yuval Taylor

It is debatable whether Nat Turner, who incited the bloodiest slave rebellion in nineteenth-century America, was, strictly speaking, an abolitionist. Born a slave and held in bondage by several different masters, including the Travis family, whose murder he instigated, Nat Turner claimed that he was motivated not by abolitionist sentiments so much as by a mystical religious fervor. By all accounts Nat Turner was an intelligent, deeply religious man who insisted he had experienced mystical visions from very early childhood. A series of bizarre visions, combined with the "heavenly sign" of an eclipse, drove Turner to incite roughly forty other slaves to a slaughter that began with the Travis household, then spread like wildfire as the insurrectionists attacked any whites they happened upon. Some of Turner's followers were killed or captured, but many, including Turner himself, escaped and went into hiding. Turner was not apprehended until October 30, 1831; once captured, he confessed and attempted to explain his crimes.

Because little is known about Nat Turner outside of his confession, Yuval Taylor focuses the following selection on the biographical information conveyed in the document and raises the question of bias and distortion on the part of Thomas Ruffin Gray, the attorney who recorded the inter-

Yuval Taylor, "Nat Turner (1800–31)," *I Was Born a Slave: An Anthology of Classic Slave Narratives*, vol. 1, edited by Yuval Taylor. Chicago, IL: Lawrence Hill Books, 1999. Copyright © 1999 by Yuval Taylor. Reproduced by permission of the publisher.

rogation. Taylor suggests that Gray may have omitted or deliberately misinterpreted Turner's words to support a proslavery position. Yet Taylor also concludes that the combination of revolutionary and religious ardor that mark the confession were indeed Turner's, even if Gray may have downplayed the former in order to emphasize the latter.

Yuval Taylor has written and edited books on American jazz and African American history.

❦   ❦   ❦

Nat Turner (1800–31) led the deadliest slave revolt in U.S. history. In the predawn hours of August 22, 1831, this slave of the cotton and tobacco fields of southeastern Virginia, whose father had long since run away to freedom, gathered together a small band of followers who esteemed him as a prophet. Over the next forty hours, armed with axes, they killed between fifty-seven and sixty-five white men, women, and children (although Turner himself killed only one person, a white woman).

As the revolt was quashed, thousands of troops converged on Southampton County. We will never know exactly how many slaves died during the fighting and in subsequent reprisals, but some scholars estimate as many as two hundred, or about three times the number that actually participated. A cavalry company from Murfreesboro, North Carolina, slaughtered forty blacks in two days, placing fifteen of their severed heads on poles as a public warning. In a three-week period, nearly fifty slaves and free blacks were tried for participation in the rebellion; thirty of them were sentenced to death, although only nineteen were actually hanged.

Turner himself, however, escaped and remained hidden for close to six weeks. On the day after his capture,

Monday, October 31, he was questioned by two court justices, with several other witnesses present. Only sketchy accounts of this interrogation survive, but it is evident that much of what he told them he repeated or elaborated on in the interviews that resulted in the *Confessions*. However, three elements of his initial confession did not reappear there. He claimed that God had given him power over the weather and seasons, that "by the efficacy of prayer" he could cause thunderstorms or droughts, that he could heal the sick. Regarding the revolt, he stated that if he could do it all over again, "he must necessarily act in the same way." And most importantly, he explained that "indiscriminate massacre was not their intention after they obtained foothold, and was resorted to in the first instance to strike terror and alarm. Women and children would afterwards have been spared, and men too who ceased to resist."

Probably one of the men present at the questioning was an attorney named Thomas Ruffin Gray. He was born, like Turner, in 1800; in December 1830 he had become an attorney. But his last few months had been disastrous: his wife had died, leaving him an infant daughter; many of his friends, neighbors, and acquaintances were killed in the revolt; and while he was acting as a public defender for four slaves during the subsequent trials, his father died, disinheriting him. Over the space of the last two years his property had dwindled from twenty-one slaves and eight hundred acres to one slave and three hundred acres (and would dwindle still further—to one horse, no slaves, and no land—by 1832). From these facts alone, it would be reasonable to infer that Gray was a somewhat desperate man, and that the prospect of publishing the confessions of so famous a criminal would be too financially appealing to pass up.

It appears that for the following three days, November 1 through 3, Gray interviewed Turner extensively, with the explicit understanding that the result would be published as Turner's confessions. Clearly, Turner was willing to talk. As [historian] Stephen Oates conjectures, "Though Nat never said so, this would be his last opportunity to strike back at the slave world he hated, to flay it with verbal brilliance and religious prophecy (was not exhortation his forte?). Indeed, a published confession would ensure Nat a kind of immortality; it would recount his extraordinary life in his own words and on his own terms."

Nat Turner, Christlike or Diabolical?

The end result was *The Confessions of Nat Turner*, which Peter Wood has justly called "one of the most extraordinary firsthand texts in American history." It is a unique document, since it was produced by a collaboration between a slave who held whites in contempt and a slave owner who had little if any respect for blacks. Nat Turner compared himself to Christ; Thomas Gray regarded Turner as a kind of devil. For Turner, his confession, like his life, would be a revelation of Holy Scripture; for Gray, it would simply confirm that Turner was a deluded maniac. The *Confessions* presents two texts, Turner's and Gray's, working against each other, yet inseparable.

The part that is most clearly Turner's is the apocalyptic rhetoric, which in this context was nothing short of revolutionary. As the narrative of Charles Ball put it only five years later, "The idea of a revolution in the conditions of the whites and the blacks, is the cornerstone of the religion of the latter." For Turner, religion and revolution went hand in hand—it was no coincidence that the revolt was originally slated for Independence Day.

It is striking, then, that the published *Confessions* barely mentions freedom. Could Turner have failed to state to Gray his final objective? Or did Gray distort

Turner's words in order to give the impression that Turner was a fiendish madman? Although Gray was intimately familiar with every detail of the revolt, he fails to mention two vitally important facts. First, Turner was married, with two children, and he deliberately spared from bloodshed the family of his wife's owner. Second, the massacre was only the first step in a much bigger plan. These omissions make it easier for Gray to paint Turner as a lone fanatic rather than a family man and revolutionary thinker, and in doing so to implicitly justify rather than condemn the institution of slavery.

Omissions and Distortions

The omissions go hand in hand with other self-serving distortions. The excerpt from the trial that appears at the end of the *Confessions* bears little resemblance to the trial transcript. The confession that was read at the trial appears to be the one taken by the justices on October 31, not the one given to Gray; Turner probably did not state that he had "made a full confession to Mr. Gray"; and the justice's final speech in the *Confessions* was clearly embellished, if not wholly fabricated, by Gray.

In addition, Gray attributes to Turner certain words that Turner was unlikely to have uttered. He has Turner say, "a circumstance occurred which . . . laid the ground work of that enthusiasm, which has terminated so fatally to many, both white and black, and for which I am about to atone at the gallows." Yet it is clear from the rest of the *Confessions*, from accounts of the interview with the justices, and from Turner's plea of not guilty at his trial, that he felt no remorse for the killings; and he hardly would have belittled his religious convictions as an "enthusiasm." Turner's account of the killings is replete with phrases that were most likely inserted by Gray: "but it was only to sleep the sleep of death"; "Vain hope!"; "to an untimely grave"; "[I] viewed the mangled bodies as they lay, in silent satisfaction"; "to arrest the progress of these barbarous villains"; "we found no more victims to gratify our thirst for blood."

Yet one can also infer that the majority of Turner's confession remains intact, for its details are very close to those of the justices' interrogation. In addition, Gray does not censor or simplify Nat's accounts of his own intelligence, his black rage, his complex and audacious interpretation of Scripture, or his faithfulness to it. According to Eric Sundquist, this interpretation "makes Christ a typological prefiguring of [Turner], the slave rebel. . . . In Turner's prophecy slavery is the Antichrist, Revelation is equivalent to revolution, and he is the Redeemer whose acts of chastening, completed by martyrdom, will inaugurate the holy utopia. . . . In the moment of the eclipse, Turner became the black Christ of the South." Gray allows Turner to present this prophecy without denying the scriptural basis for Turner's significance in this world. Instead, as William Andrews notes, "The lawyer simply tries to counter Turner's view of himself as Savior with an opposing estimate of him as Satanically inspired. This in itself constitutes a rhetorical victory for Turner."

The Rebellion's Harsh Consequences

But this victory was posthumous. At his trial on November 5, the judge pronounced Turner guilty as charged and asked if he had anything to say before sentencing. "Nothing but what I've said before," he replied. He went to his execution six days later bravely and with his head up. According to interviews conducted in 1900 by William Sidney Drewry, "Nat Turner's body was delivered to the doctors, who skinned it and made grease of the flesh. His skeleton was for many years in the possession of Dr. Massenberg, but has since been misplaced. . . . Mr. R.S. Barham's father owned a money purse made of his hide." As Kenneth Greenberg comments, "Apparently unaware of the bizarre mixture of horror and irony in their actions, Southampton whites consumed the body and the blood of the black rebel who likened himself to Christ."

"It would be difficult to exaggerate the psychic toll which the Turner massacre exacted from the southern mind," write Seymour Gross and Eileen Bender. "As is evidenced in the ritualistic desecration of Turner's body, the event had cut through to the lower layers of the psyche where the nightmares are transacted." In addition to barbarous reprisals and paralyzing fear, this was evident in new Virginia laws prohibiting blacks, both slave and free, from preaching or conducting religious meetings and from learning to read or write. And throughout the South abolitionist literature was seized and burned. In the North, on the other hand, Turner's revolt helped catalyze three decades of increased abolitionist agitation.

The Impact of the Confessions

Incendiary as it was, *The Confessions of Nat Turner* found singular success in both North and South. Gray had produced it extraordinarily quickly, copyrighting it on November 10 and publishing it less than two weeks later. Thomas Wentworth Higginson, writing in 1861, estimated that fifty thousand copies had been sold, although he later revised that estimate to forty thousand. It was reprinted in Virginia in 1832, and went through at least five editions in the nineteenth century.

Although the legend of Nat Turner has been supplemented by a great deal of myth-making, the *Confessions* has been the basis for almost all that has been written about him and his revolt. Harriet Beecher Stowe was one writer who was fascinated by Turner, and based her 1856 novel *Dred* on the *Confessions*, which she appended to it. More recently, William Styron entitled his controversial 1967 novel *The Confessions of Nat Turner*, as if he were attempting to supplant the original. And Stephen B. Oates's highly acclaimed 1975 biography, *The Fires of Jubilee*, also owes its primary debt to the *Confessions*. As Sundquist eloquently notes, "in the enigmatic Scripture he left in the wake of his uprising, Turner continued his confession in a dimension certain to outlast the historical moment of his death."

Confessions of an Insurrectionist

Nat Turner

Regardless of the uncertain motives of its leader, the Nat Turner insurrection became a rallying point in the slavery controversy. The incident seemed to confirm the worst prejudices and fears of proslavery advocates, for many proving their claim that blacks were subhuman, barbaric, inherently dangerous, and thus suited only to strict bondage. For the abolitionist movement, just coming into full bloom with the appearance of William Lloyd Garrison's antislavery newspaper the *Liberator*, the Turner rebellion ignited a passionate debate over whether violence was justifiable and perhaps even necessary in order to achieve emancipation. Many white abolitionists were Quakers firmly committed to the idea of peaceful resistance. Publisher Garrison disdained even using the political process for the aims of abolition. But some radical black abolitionists such as David Walker and Henry Highland Garnet endorsed all means, including violence, in the struggle for freedom, reasoning that white slave interests were unlikely to agree to emancipation unless coerced. While eminent leaders such as Frederick Douglass attempted to distance themselves somewhat from their more revolutionary black abolitionist brethren, the radicals rather than the moderates were ultimately proven correct: the Civil War made

Thomas R. Gray, *The Confessions of Nat Turner, the Leader of the Late Insurrection, in Southhampton (County)*. Baltimore, 1831.

tragically clear the fact that slavery would end only by bloodshed. Did Nat Turner realize that his insurrection would intensify the political, moral, and sectional divisions overtaking the nation? The answer is unclear. The following selection, excerpted from Turner's confession, supports the notion that Turner's actions were driven by a kind of religious mania rather than by the extreme duress of slavery. However, it is important to keep in mind the fact that the confession was transcribed by Thomas Ruffin Gray, a white Virginian, and that the characterization of Turner as an irrational religious fanatic might well have served the interests of a frightened white populace reluctant to fan the flames of abolitionism.

🦋 🦋 🦋

I was thirty-one years of age the second of October last, and born the property of Benjamin Turner, of this county. In my childhood a circumstance occurred which made an indelible impression on my mind, and laid the groundwork of that enthusiasm which has terminated so fatally to many, both white and black, and for which I am about to atone at the gallows. It is here necessary to relate this circumstance. Trifling as it may seem, it was the commencement of that belief which has grown with time; and even now, sir, in his dungeon, helpless and forsaken as I am, I cannot divest myself of. Being at play with other children, when three or four years old, I was telling them something, which my mother, overhearing, said it had happened before I was born. I stuck to my story, however, and related some things which went, in her opinion, to confirm it. Others being called on, were greatly astonished, knowing that these things had happened, and caused them to say, in my hearing, I surely would be a prophet, as the Lord had shown me things that had happened before my birth. And my mother and grandmother strengthened me in this my first impression, saying, in my presence, I was intended for some great purpose, which they had always thought from certain marks on my head and breast. . . .

A Mind Unsuited to Slavery

My grandmother, who was very religious, and to whom I was much attached—my master, who belonged to the church, and other religious persons who visited the house, and whom I often saw at prayers, noticing the singularity of my manners, I suppose, and my uncommon intelligence for a child, remarked I had too much sense to be raised, and, if I was, I would never be of any service to any one as a slave. To a mind like mine, restless, inquisitive, and observant of everything that was passing, it is easy to suppose that religion was the subject to which it would be directed; and, although this subject principally occupied my thoughts, there was nothing that I saw or heard of to which my attention was not directed. The manner in which I learned to read and write, not only had great influence on my own mind, as I acquired it with the most perfect ease—so much so, that I have no recollection whatever of learning the alphabet; but, to the astonishment of the family, one day, when a book was shown me, to keep me from crying, I began spelling the names of different objects. This was a source of wonder to all in the neighborhood, particularly the blacks—and this learning was constantly improved at all opportunities. When I got large enough to go to work, while employed I was reflecting on many things that would present themselves to my imagination; and whenever an opportunity occurred of looking at a book, when the school-children were getting their lessons, I would find many things that the fertility of my own imagination had depicted to me before. All my time, not devoted to my master's service, was spent either in prayer, or in making experiments in casting different things in moulds made of earth, in attempting to make paper, gunpowder, and many other experiments, that, although I could not perfect, yet convinced me of its practicability if I had the means.

I was not addicted to stealing in my youth, nor have ever been; yet such was the confidence of the Negroes in the neighborhood, even at this early period of my life, in my superior judgment, that they would often carry me with them when they were going on any roguery, to plan for them. Growing up among them with this confidence in my superior judgment, and when this, in their opinions, was perfected by Divine inspiration, from the circumstances already alluded to in my infancy, and which belief was ever afterwards zealously inculcated by the austerity of my life and manners, which became the subject of remark by white and black; having soon discovered to be great, I must appear so, and therefore studiously avoided mixing in society, and wrapped myself in mystery, devoting my time to fasting and prayer.

A Divine Purpose

By this time, having arrived to man's estate, and hearing the Scriptures commented on at meetings, I was struck with that particular passage which says, "Seek ye the kingdom of heaven, and all things shall be added unto you." I reflected much on this passage, and prayed daily for light on this subject. As I was praying one day at my plough, the Spirit spoke to me, saying, "Seek ye the kingdom of heaven, and all things shall be added unto you." Question. "What do you mean by the Spirit?" Answer. "The Spirit that spoke to the prophets in former days, and I was greatly astonished, and for two years prayed continually, whenever my duty would permit; and then again I had the same revelation, which fully confirmed me in the impression that I was ordained for some great purpose in the hands of the Almighty. Several years rolled round, in which many events occurred to strengthen me in this my belief. At this time I reverted in my mind to the remarks made of me in my childhood, and the things that had been shown me; and as it had been said of me in my childhood, by those by whom I had been taught to pray, both white and black, and in whom I had the greatest confidence, that I had too much sense to be raised, and if I was I would never be of any use to any one as a slave; now, finding I had arrived to man's estate, and was a slave, and these revelations being made known to me, I began to direct my attention to this great object, to fulfil the purpose for which, by this time, I felt assured I was intended. Knowing the influence I had obtained over the minds of my fellow-servants (not by the means of conjuring and such like tricks—for to them I always spoke of such things with contempt), but by the communion of the Spirit, whose revelations I often communicated to them, and they believed and said my wisdom came from God,—I now began to prepare them for my purpose, by telling them something was about to happen that would terminate in fulfilling the great promise that had been made to me.

More Messages and Visions
About this time I was placed under an overseer, from whom I ran away, and after remaining in the woods thirty days, I returned, to the astonishment of the Negroes on the plantation, who thought I had made my escape to some other part of the country, as my father had done before. But the reason of my return was, that the Spirit appeared to me and said I had my wishes directed to the things of this world, and not to the kingdom of

heaven, and that I should return to the service of my earthly master—"For he who knoweth his Master's will, and doeth it not, shall be beaten with many stripes, and thus have I chastened you." And the Negroes found fault, and murmured against me, saying that if they had my sense they would not serve any master in the world. And about this time I had a vision—and I saw white spirits and black spirits engaged in battle, and the sun was darkened—the thunder rolled in the heavens, and blood flowed in streams—and I heard a voice saying, "Such is your luck, such you are called to see; and let it come rough or smooth, you must surely bear it."

I now withdrew myself as much as my situation would permit from the intercourse of my fellow-servants, for the avowed purpose of serving the Spirit more fully; and it appeared to me, and reminded me of the things it had already shown me, and that it would then reveal to me the knowledge of the elements, the revolution of the planets, the operation of tides, and changes of the seasons. After this revelation in the year 1825, and the knowledge of the elements being made known to me, I sought more than ever to obtain true holiness before the great day of judgment should appear, and then I began to receive the true knowledge of faith. And from the first steps of righteousness until the last, was I made perfect; and the Holy Ghost was with me, and said, "Behold me as I stand in the heavens." And I looked and saw the forms of men in different attitudes; and there were lights in the sky, to which the children of darkness gave other names what they really were; for they were the lights of the Saviour's hands, stretched forth from east to west, even as they were extended on the cross on Calvary for the redemption of sinners. And I wondered greatly at these miracles, and prayed to be informed of a certainty of the meaning thereof; and shortly afterwards, while laboring in the field, I discovered drops of blood on the corn, as though it were dew from heaven; and I communicated it to many, both white and black, in the neighborhood—and I then found on the leaves in the woods hieroglyphic characters and numbers, with the forces of men in different attitudes, portrayed in blood, and representing the figures I had seen before in the heavens. And now the Holy Ghost had revealed itself to me, and made plain the miracles it had shown me; for as the blood of Christ had been shed on this earth, and had ascended to heaven for the salvation of sinners, and was now returning to earth again in the form of dew,—and as the leaves on the trees bore the impression of the figures I had seen in the heavens,—it was plain to me that the Saviour was about to lay down the yoke he had borne for the sins of men, and the great day of judgment was at hand.

The Spirit Exhorts the Uprising

About this time I told these things to a white man (Etheldred T. Brantley), on whom it had a wonderful effect; and he ceased from his wickedness, and was attacked immediately with a cutaneous eruption, and blood oozed from the pores of his skin, and after praying and fasting nine days he was healed. And the Spirit appeared to me again, and said, as the Saviour had been baptized, so should we be also; and when the white people would not let us be baptized by the church, we went down into the water together, in the sight of many who reviled us, and were baptized by the Spirit. After this I rejoiced greatly, and gave thanks to God. And on the 12th of May, 1828, I heard a loud noise in the heavens, and the Spirit instantly appeared to me and said the Serpent was loosened, and Christ had laid down the yoke he had borne for the sins of men, and that I should take it on and fight against the Serpent, for the time was fast approaching when the first should be last and the last should be first. . . . And by signs in the heavens that it would make known to me when I should commence the great work, and until the first sign appeared I should conceal it from the knowledge of men; and on the appearance of the sign (the eclipse of the sun, last February), I should arise and prepare myself, and slay my enemies with their own weapons. And immediately on the sign appearing in the heavens, the seal was removed from my lips, and I communicated the great work laid out for me to do, to four in whom I had the greatest confidence (Henry, Hark, Nelson, and Sam). It was intended by us to have begun the work of death on the 4th of July last. Many were the plans formed and rejected by us, and it affected my mind to such a degree that I fell sick, and the time passed without our coming to any determination how to commence—still forming new schemes and rejecting them, when the sign appeared again, which determined me not to wait longer.

The Plans Take Shape

Since the commencement of 1830 I had been living with Mr. Joseph Travis, who was to me a kind master, and placed the greatest confidence in me; in fact, I had no cause to complain of his treatment to me. On Saturday evening, the 20th of August, it was agreed between Henry, Hark, and myself, to prepare a dinner the next day for the men we expected, and then to concert a plan, as we had not yet determined on any. Hark, on the following morning, brought a pig, and Henry brandy; and being joined by Sam, Nelson, Will, and Jack, they prepared in the woods a dinner, where, about three o'clock, I joined them.

Q. [Asked by Turner's interrogator] Why were you so backward in joining them?

A. The same reason that had caused me not to mix

with them years before, I saluted them on coming up, and asked Will how came he there. He answered, his life was worth no more than others, and his liberty as dear to him. I asked him if he thought to obtain it. He said he would, or lose his life. This was enough to put him in full confidence. Jack, I knew, was only a tool in the hands of Hark. It was quickly agreed we should commence at home (Mr. J. Travis) on that night; and until we had armed and equipped ourselves, and gathered sufficient force, neither age nor sex was to be spared—which was invariably adhered to. We remained at the feast until about two hours in the night, when we went to the house and found Austin. . . .

Terror and Devastation

I took my station in the rear, and, as it was my object to carry terror and devastation wherever we went, I placed fifteen or twenty of the best armed and most to be relied on in front, who generally approached the houses as fast as their horses could run. This was for two purposes—to prevent their escape, and strike terror to the inhabitants; on this account I never got to the houses, after leaving Mrs. Whitehead's, until the murders were committed, except in one case. I sometimes got in sight in time to see the work of death completed; viewed the mangled bodies as they lay, in silent satisfaction, and immediately started in quest of other victims. Having murdered Mrs. Waller and ten children, we started for Mr. Wm. Williams,—having killed him and two little boys that were there; while engaged in this, Mrs. Williams fled and got some distance from the house, but she was pursued, overtaken, and compelled to get up behind one of the company, who brought her back, and, after showing her the mangled body of her lifeless husband, she was told to get down and lay by his side, where she was shot dead.

The white men pursued and fired on us several times. Hark had his horse shot under him, and I caught another for him as it was running by me; five or six of my men were wounded, but none left on the field. Finding myself defeated here, I instantly determined to go through a private way, and cross the Nottoway River at the Cypress Bridge, three miles below Jerusalem, and attack that place in the rear, as I expected they would look for me on the other road, and I had a great desire to get there to procure arms and ammunition. After going a short distance in this private way, accompanied by about twenty men, I overtook two or three, who told me the others were dispersed in every direction. On this, I gave up all hope for the present; and on Thursday night, after having supplied myself with provisions from Mr. Travis, I scratched a hole under a pile of fence-rails in a field, where I concealed myself for six weeks, never leaving my hiding-place but for a few minutes in the dead of the night to get water, which was very near. Thinking by this time I could venture out, I began to go about in the night, and eavesdrop the houses in the neighborhood—pursuing this course for about a fortnight, and gathering little or no intelligence, afraid of speaking to any human being, and returning every morning to my cave before the dawn of day. I know not how long I might have led this life, if accident had not betrayed me. A dog in the neighborhood passing by my hiding-place one night while I was out, was attracted by some meat I had in my cave, and crawled in and stole it, and was coming out just as I returned. A few nights after, two Negroes having started to go hunting with the same dog, and passed that way, the dog came again to the place, and having just gone out to walk about, discovered me and barked; on which, thinking myself discovered, I spoke to them to beg concealment. On making myself known, they fled from me. Knowing then they would betray me, I immediately left my hiding-place, and was pursued almost incessantly, until I was taken, a fortnight afterwards, by Mr. Benjamin Phipps, in a little hole I had dug out with my sword, for the purpose of concealment, under the top of a fallen tree.

During the time I was pursued, I had many hairbreadth escapes, which your time will not permit you to relate. I am here loaded with chains, and willing to suffer the fate that awaits me.

Maria Stewart

William S. Parsons and Margaret A. Drew

Teacher, reformer, writer, and abolitionist, Maria Stewart
was a pioneer both for her race and her gender. She was
the first-known black woman to deliver a public address in
the United States and, as William S. Parsons and Margaret
A. Drew observe in the following profile, likely the first
American woman of any race to do so. Parsons and Drew
also examine Stewart's early life as a house servant, her passionate involvement in the abolitionist movement, and her
strong religious convictions that guided her work as activist
and educator.

William S. Parsons is a scholar and curator of Holocaust
and African American history. Since 1996 he has served as
chief of staff of the U.S. Holocaust Museum. Like Parsons,
Margaret A. Drew has published extensively on African
American and Holocaust history.

🐝 🐝 🐝

Although Maria Stewart's career as a public figure
lasted less than three years, she earned her place in the
history of black Americans by being the first black
woman, and probably the first native-born American
woman, to speak in public and leave texts of her

speeches. Born in Hartford, Connecticut in 1803, as Maria Miller, she was orphaned when she was five years old. Most of her youth, until she was fifteen, was spent as a servant in the home of a minister. After that she attended "Sabbath schools" until she was twenty, and worked as a domestic servant until she married James W. Stewart. Their wedding took place on August 10, 1826, with the Rev. Thomas Paul, the minister of the African Meeting House, performing the service.

James Stewart, several years older than Maria, was a Boston shipping agent, probably the only black shipping agent in Boston. The marriage lasted only three years. In 1829, Stewart became ill and died. The inheritance that should have gone to Maria upon his death was wiped out through the deceit of a group of white businessmen. Her grief at her husband's death was compounded by a two-year legal battle over this legacy.

The Influence of David Walker and William Lloyd Garrison

The death of David Walker, in 1830, only a year after her husband's death further deepened her grief. Stewart, always strongly religious, had also been influenced by Walker, the author of a fiery black manifesto. Stewart's first manuscript was written following Walker's death, an essay entitled "Religion and the Pure Principles of Morality, The Sure Foundation on Which We Must Build." In it she refers to Walker as well as to William Lloyd Garrison: "God hath raised you up a Walker and a Garrison. Though Walker sleeps, yet he lives, and his name shall be had in everlasting remembrance."

In 1831, Stewart went to Garrison with her manuscript which he published in pamphlet form. Her words were addressed to a black audience. She urged them not to "kill, burn, or destroy" but to "improve your talents . . . show forth your powers of mind." Reminding her readers that both God and the Constitution declared them equal with other men, she said, "It is not the color of the skin that makes the man, but it is the principles formed within the soul." Addressing herself specifically to black women, she said, "O, ye daughters of Africa, awake! Awake! Arise! No longer sleep nor slumber, but distinguish yourselves. Show forth to the world that ye are endowed with noble and exalted faculties."

While acknowledging that America had done little to encourage blacks to develop their talents, she placed the burden for changing this squarely on the shoulders of blacks themselves—". . .'I can't,' is a great barrier in the way. I hope it will soon be removed, and 'I will,' resume its place." Later she added, "It is of no use for us to sit with our hands folded, hanging our heads like bulrushed, lamenting our wretched condition; but let us make a mighty effort, and arise; and if no one will promote or respect us, let us promote and respect ourselves."

Maria Stewart, Public Speaker

The following year, 1832, Stewart published a collection of religious meditations. During 1832 and 1833 she delivered four public lectures, portions of which were also published in *The Liberator*. In the third of these speeches, delivered at the African Masonic Hall in Boston, she made her feelings clear about the American Colonization Society and its attempts to encourage blacks to return to Africa. . . .

The last of Stewart's early speeches was her Farewell Address as she prepared to leave Boston. The speech was delivered on September 21, 1833, in the school room at the African Meeting House, known at that time as the Belknap Street Church. Her speech reflected her discouragement with regard to her public life in Boston and hinted at the opposition she had received, some of which may have been due to the strong religious tone of her speeches and writings. Her reasons for feeling discouraged were confirmed by William C. Nell in a letter written to Garrison almost twenty years after Maria Stewart left Boston, where he stated that "her sentiments on the improvement of colored Americans, encountered an opposition even from her Boston circle of friends, that would have dampened the ardor of most women."

Life After Boston

When Stewart left Boston, she went first to New York. It was there, in 1835, that she published her collected works. In New York, she taught school and participated in women's anti-slavery and literary organizations. She also taught for a time in Baltimore before settling in Washington, D.C. after the Civil War. She was eventually to become Matron of the Freedmen's Hospital in Washington, now known as the Howard University hospital.

She returned to Boston at least once, about 1878 or 1879. Congress had recently passed a bill that entitled her to a pension as the widow of a veteran of the War of 1812. She came to Boston to get the necessary papers to prove that she qualified for her pension. While in Boston she had a reunion with Garrison whom she had not seen for many years. Later that year she published a new edition of her collected works accompanied by an autobiographical sketch. She died in 1879.

Black Americans Are Entitled to Freedom

Maria Stewart

Maria Stewart's presence at Boston's African Masonic Hall February 27, 1833, was doubly scandalous: Not only was she a woman daring to deliver a public speech, but her audience was composed of both sexes in defiance of rigid early-nineteenth-century social protocol. Characteristically, Stewart's address combines a passionate condemnation of slavery and racial oppression with equally heartfelt religious fervor and commitment to social reform. She chides the people of the free black community—especially the youth—for allowing themselves to be distracted from the righteous pursuit of liberty and self-improvement by such frivolous activities as gambling and dancing, urging them to rise up and demand the emancipation of slaves and equal rights for all. But she also warns the white America that forces blacks—free and enslaved—into servitude that God's wrath may strike at them through the "sons and daughters of Africa." As proud of her people's noble African heritage as she is opposed to the notion of colonization or forced emigration, Stewart emphatically represents herself as an African American.

Maria Stewart, address delivered at the African Masonic Hall, Boston, MA, February 27, 1833.

❧ ❧ ❧

African rights and liberty is a subject that ought to fire the breast of every free man of color in these United States, and excite in his bosom a lively, deep, decided and heart-felt interest. When I cast my eyes on the long list of illustrious names that are enrolled on the bright annals of fame among the whites, I turn my eyes within, and ask my thoughts, "Where are the names of *our* illustrious ones?" It must certainly have been for the want of energy on the part of the free people of color, that they have been long willing to bear the yoke of oppression. It must have been the want of ambition and force that has given the whites occasion to say, that our natural abilities are not as good, and our capacities by nature inferior to theirs. They boldly assert, that, did we possess a natural independence of soul, and feel a love for liberty within our breasts, some one of our sable race, long before this, would have testified it, notwithstanding the disadvantages under which we labor. We have made ourselves appear altogether unqualified to speak in our own defence, and are therefore looked upon as objects of pity and commiseration. We have been imposed upon, insulted and derided on every side; and now, if we complain, it is considered as the height of impertinence. We have suffered ourselves to be considered as Bastards, cowards, mean, faint-hearted wretches; and on this account, (not because of our complexion) many despise us, and would gladly spurn us from their presence.

Knowledge Is Power

These things have fired my soul with a holy indignation, and compelled me thus to come forward; and endeavor to turn their attention to knowledge and improvement; for knowledge is power. I would ask, is it blindness of mind, or at stupidity of soul, or the want of education, that has caused our men who are 60 to 70 years of age, never to let their voices be heard, or nor their hands be raised in behalf of their color? Or has it been for the fear of offending the whites? If it has, O ye fearful ones, throw off your fearfulness, and come forth in the name of the Lord, and in the strength of the God of Justice, and make yourselves useful and active members in society; for they admire a noble and patriotic spirit in others; and should they not admire it in us? If you are men, convince them that you possess the spirit of men; and as your day, so shall your strength be. Have the sons of Africa no souls? feel they no ambitious desires? shall the chains of ignorance forever confine them? shall the insipid appellation of "clever negroes," or "good creatures," any longer content them? Where can we find among ourselves the man of science, or a philosopher, or an able statesman, or a counsellor at law? Show me our fearless and brave, our noble and gallant ones. Where are our lecturers on natural history, and our critics in useful knowledge? There may be a few such men among us, but they are rare. It is true, our fathers bled and died in the revolutionary war, and others fought bravely under the command of [Andrew] Jackson, in defence of liberty. But where is the man that has distinguished himself in these modern days by acting wholly in the defence of African rights and liberty? There was one, although he sleeps, his memory lives.

I am sensible that there are many highly intelligent gentlemen of color in those United States, in the force of whose arguments, doubtless, I should discover my inferiority; but if they are blest with wit and talent, friends and fortune, why have they not made themselves men of eminence, by striving to take all the reproach that is cast upon the people of color, and in endeavoring to alleviate the woes of their brethren in bondage? Talk, without effort, is nothing; you are abundantly capable, gentlemen, of making yourselves men of distinction; and this gross neglect, on your part, causes my blood to boil within me. Here is the grand cause which hinders the rise and progress of the people of color. It is their want of laudable ambition and requisite courage.

The Greatness of African Heritage

Individuals have been distinguished according to their genius and talents, ever since the first formation of man, and will continue to be while the world stands. The different grades rise to honor and respectability as their merits may deserve. History informs us that we sprung from one of the most learned nations of the whole earth; from the seat, if not the parent of science; yes, poor, despised Africa was once the resort of sages and legislators of other nations, was esteemed the school for learning, and the most illustrious men in Greece flocked thither for instruction. But it was our gross sins and abominations that provoked the Almighty to frown thus heavily upon us, and give our glory unto others. Sin and prodigality have caused the downfall of nations, kings and emperors; and were it not that God in wrath remembers mercy; we might indeed despair; but a promise is left us; "Ethiopia shall again stretch forth her hands unto God."

But it is of no use for us to boast that we sprung from this learned and enlightened nation, for this day a thick mist of moral gloom hangs over millions of our race. Our condition as a people has been low for hundreds of years, and it will continue to be so, unless, by true piety and virtue, we strive to regain that which we have lost. White Americans, by their prudence, economy and exertions, have sprung up and become one of the most flourishing nations in the world, distinguished for their knowledge of the arts and sciences, for their polite literature. While our minds are vacant, and starving for want of knowledge, theirs are filled to overflowing. Most of our color have been taught to stand in fear of the white man, from their earliest infancy, to work as soon as they could walk, and call "master," before they scarce could lisp the name of *mother*. Continual fear and laborious servitude have in some degree lessened in us that natural force and energy which belong to man; or else, in defiance of opposition, our men, before this, would have nobly and boldly contended for their rights. But give the man of color an equal opportunity with the white from the cradle to manhood, and from manhood to the grave, and you would discover the dignified statesman, the man of science, and the philosopher. But there is no such opportunity for the sons of Africa, and I fear that our powerful one's are fully determined that there never shall be. Forbid, ye Powers on high, that it should any longer be said that our men possess no force. O ye sons of Africa, when will your voices be heard in our legislative halls, in defiance of your enemies, contending for equal rights and liberty? How can you, when you reflect from what you have fallen, refrain from crying mightily unto God, to turn away from us the fierceness of his anger, and remember our transgressions against us no more forever. But a God of infinite purity will not regard the prayers of those who hold religion in one hand, and prejudice, sin and pollution in the other; he will not regard the prayers of self-righteousness and hypocrisy.

Is it possible, I exclaim, that for the want of knowledge, we have labored for hundreds of years to support others, and been content to receive what they chose to give us in return? Cast your eyes about, look as far as you can see; all, all is owned by the lordly white, except here and there a lowly dwelling which the man of color, midst deprivations, fraud and opposition, has been scarce able to procure. Like king Solomon, who put neither nail nor hammer to the temple, yet received the praise; so also have the white Americans gained themselves a name, like the names of the great men that are in the earth, while in reality we have been their principal foundation and support. We have pursued the shadow, they have obtained the substance; we have performed the labor, they have received the profits; we have planted the vines, they have eaten the fruits of them.

The Importance of Self-Improvement and Temperance

I would implore our men, and especially our rising youth, to flee from the gambling board and the dance-hall; for we are poor, and have no money to throw away. I do not consider dancing as criminal in itself, but it is astonishing to me that our young men are so blind to their own interest and the future welfare of their children, as to spend their hard earnings for this frivolous amusement; for it has been carried on among us to such an unbecoming extent, that it has became absolutely disgusting. "Faithful are the wounds of a friend, but the kisses of an enemy are deceitful." Had those men among us, who have had an opportunity, turned their attention as assiduously to mental and moral improvement as they have to gambling and dancing, I might have remained quietly at home, and they stood contending in my place. These polite accomplishments will never enroll your names on the bright annals of time, who admire the belle void of intellectual knowledge, or applaud the dandy that talks largely on politics, without striving to assist his fellow in the revolution, when the nerves and muscles of every other man forced him into the field of action. You have a right to rejoice, and to let your hearts cheer you in the days of your youth; yet remember that for all these things, God will bring you into judgment. Then, O ye sons of Africa, turn your mind from these perishable objects, and contend for the cause of God and the rights of man. Form yourselves into temperance societies. There are temperate men among you; then why will you any longer neglect to strive, by your example, to suppress vice in all its abhorrent forms? You have been told repeatedly of the glorious results arising from temperance, and can you bear to see the whites arising in honor and respectability, without endeavoring to grasp after that honor and respectability also?

But I forbear. Let our money, instead of being thrown away as heretofore, be appropriated for schools and seminaries of learning for our children and youth. We ought to follow the example of the whites in this respect. Nothing would raise our respectability, add to our peace and happiness, and reflect so much honor upon us, as to be ourselves the promoters of temperance, and the supporters, as far as we are able, of useful and scientific knowledge. The rays of light and knowledge have been hid from our view; we have been taught to consider ourselves as scarce superior to the brute creation; and have performed the most laborious part of American drugery. Had we as a people received, one half the early advantages the whites have received, I would defy the government of these United States to deprive us any longer of our rights.

Colonization and White Prejudice

I am informed that the agent of the Colonization Society has recently formed an association of young men, for the purpose of influencing those of us to go to Liberia who may feel disposed. The colonizationists are blind to their own interest, for should the nations of the earth make war with America, they would find their forces much weakened by our absence; or should we remain here, can our "brave soldiers," and "fellow-citizens," as they were termed in time of calamity, condescend to defend the rights of the whites, and be again deprived of their own, or sent to Liberia in return? Or, if the colonizationists are real friends to Africa, let them expend the money which they collect, in erecting a college to educate her injured sons in this land of gospel light and liberty; for it would be most thankfully received on our part, and convince us of the truth of their professions, and save time, expense and anxiety. Let them place before us noble objects, worthy of pursuit, and see if we prove ourselves to be those unambitious negroes they term us. But ah! methinks their hearts are so frozen towards us, they had rather their money should be sunk in the ocean than to administer it to our relief; and I fear, if they dared, like Pharaoh, king of Egypt, they would order every male child among us to be drowned. But the most high God is still as able to subdue the lofty pride of these white Americans, as He was the heart of that ancient rebel. They say, though we are looked upon as things, yet we sprang from a scientific people. Had our men the requisite force and energy, they would soon convince them by their efforts both in public and private, that they were men, or things in the shape of men. Well may the colonizationists laugh us to scorn for our negligence; well may they cry, "Shame to the sons of Africa." As the burden of the Israelites was too great for Moses to bear, . . . so also is our burden too great for our noble advocate to bear. You must feel interested, my brethren, in what he undertakes, and hold up his hands by your good works, or in spite of himself, his soul will become discouraged, and his heart will die within him; for he has, as it were, the strong bulls of Bashan to contend with.

Black Americans Must Demand Their Rights

It is of no use for us to wait any longer for a generation of well educated men to arise. We have slumbered and slept too long already; the day is far spent; the night of death approaches; and you have sound sense and good judgement sufficient to begin with, if you feel disposed to make a right use of it. Let every man of color throughout the United States, who possesses the spirit and principles of a man, sign a petition to Congress, to abolish slavery in the District of Columbia, and grant you the rights and privileges of common free citizens; for if you had had faith as a grain of mustard seed, long before this the mountains of prejudice might have been removed. We are all sensible that the Anti-Slavery Society has taken hold of the arm of our whole population, in order to raise them out of the mire. Now all we have to do is, by a spirit of virtuous ambition to strive to raise ourselves; and I am happy to have it in my power thus publicly to say, that the colored inhabitants of this city, in some respects, are beginning to improve. Had the free people of color in these United States nobly and boldly contended for their rights, and showed a natural genius and talent, although not so brilliant as some; had they held up, encouraged and patronized each other, nothing could have hindered us from being a thriving and flourishing people. There has been a fault among us. The reason why our distinguished men have not made themselves more influential is, because they fear that the strong current of opposition through which they must pass, would cause their downfall and prove their overthrow. And what gives rise to this opposition? Envy. And what has it amounted to? Nothing. And who are the cause of it? Our whited sepulchers, who want to be great, and don't know how; who love to be called of men Rabbi, Rabbi, who put on false sanctity, and humble themselves to their brethren, for the sake of acquiring the highest place in the synagogue, and the uppermost seats at the feast. You, dearly beloved, who are the genuine followers of our Lord Jesus Christ, the salt of the earth and the light of the world, are not so culpable. As I told you, in the very first of my writing, I tell you again, I am but as a drop in the bucket—as one particle of the small dust of the earth. God will surely raise up those among us who will plead the cause of virtue, and the pure principles of morality, more eloquently than I am able to do.

America Is Another Babylon

It appears to me that America has become like the great city of Babylon, for she has boasted in her heart,—I sit a queen, and am no widow, and shall see no sorrow? She is indeed a seller of slaves and the souls of men; she has made the Africans drunk with the wine of her fornication; she has put them completely beneath her feet, and she means to keep them there; her right hand supports the reins of government, and her left hand the wheel of power, and she is determined not to let go her grasp. But many powerful sons and daughters of Africa will shortly arise, who will put down vice and immorality among us, and declare by Him that sitteth upon the throne, that they will have their rights; and if refused, I am afraid they will spread horror and devastation around. I believe that the oppression of injured Africa has come up before the Majesty of Heaven; and when our cries shall have reached the ears of the Most High, it will be a tremendous day for the people of this land; for strong is the arm of the Lord God Almighty.

Life has almost lost its charms for me; death has lost its sting and the grave its terrors; and at times I have a strong desire to depart and dwell with Christ, which is far better. Let me entreat my white brethren to awake and save our sons from dissipation, and our daughters from ruin. Lend the hand of assistance to feeble merit, plead the cause of virtue among our sable race; so shall our curses upon you be turned into blessings; and though you should endeavor to drive us from these shores, still we will cling to you the more firmly; nor will we attempt to rise above you: we will presume to be called your equals only.

The unfriendly whites first drove the native American from his much loved home. Then they stole our fathers from their peaceful and quiet dwellings, and brought them hither, and made bond-men and bond-women of them and their little ones; they have obliged our brethren to labor, kept them in utter ignorance, nourished them in vice, and raised them in degradation; and now that we have enriched their soil, and filled their coffers, they say that we are not capable of becoming like white men, and that we never can rise to respectability in this country. They would drive us to a strange land. But before I go, the bayonet shall pierce me through. African rights and liberty is a subject that ought to fire the breast of every free man of color in these United States, and excite in his bosom a lively, deep, decided and heart-felt interest.

Henry "Box" Brown, Escape Artist and Abolitionist

Richard Newman

Henry "Box" Brown adopted his middle name from his unusual means of escaping slavery: he had himself shipped in a crate from Richmond to Philadelphia. The ingenuity of his successful ruse made his escape memoir, *The Narrative of the Life of Henry Box Brown*, among the most popular of the genre and drew large audiences to Brown's lectures on the abolitionist public-speaking circuit. Although Frederick Douglass disapproved of Brown's decision to publicize his remarkable mode of escape lest it alert bounty hunters to other slaves attempting a similar ploy, Brown made good use of his celebrity. He both promoted the antislavery cause in the North and in England and carved out a new living for himself as a free man as the following selection by Richard Newman describes.

Richard Newman is the fellows and research officer at Harvard University's W.E.B. Du Bois Institute for Afro-American Research. He has published widely on African American studies. His works include *Everybody Say Freedom:*

Richard Newman, *Narrative of the Life of Henry Box Brown: Written by Himself.* New York: Oxford University Press, 2002. Copyright © 2002 by Oxford University Press, Inc. Reproduced by permission.

Everything You Need to Know About African-American History and *Go Down, Moses: Celebrating the African-American Spiritual.*

❧ ❧ ❧

Of the hundreds of thousands of African-American slaves who liberated themselves by escaping from human bondage in the South, very few specific names remain with us. Most, in fact, are not even known. Some ex-slaves, however, told or wrote the stories of their lives. These narratives give us much of what we know, not only about the resistance of escape, but about slave life and thought.

One name that has not been forgotten is Henry "Box" Brown. He is stamped indelibly on the popular imagination because of his ingenious method of escape. On March 29, 1849, Brown had himself nailed inside a wooden crate and shipped via the Adams Express Co. from slavery in Richmond, Virginia, to freedom in Philadelphia, Pennsylvania. In twenty-seven hours, he traveled 350 miles, most of it in discomfort and all of it in danger.

Brown, who immediately took the name "Box" as his own, has retained the public recognition he achieved at the time of his bold flight. A black wax museum in Baltimore features a life-size Brown emerging from his packing crate. The National Park Service recommends that its site guides relate Brown's unique tale as a way to humanize any discussion of slavery, a subject most tourists apparently resist. Toyota Motors Sales Co. recently ran an advertisement telling Brown's story, picturing a large box, and "recognizing those individuals who overcame great obstacles."

The Significance of Escape Narratives

The fugitives we know are remembered primarily through their published narratives. Box Brown also issued an account of his life and escape, but his book is essentially unavailable. The first edition, published in Boston in 1849, the same year as his escape, is also highly flawed. Brown, like most other slaves, was illiterate, so his and their stories were told by sympathetic whites, more or less based on their subjects' verbal accounts. Brown's amanuensis, Charles Stearns, was perhaps the first white man to write a narrative on behalf of a slave. Stearns was such a zealous abolitionist, however, that Brown's story is spoiled by Stearns' turgid style, scolding prose, and even the addition of a polemic essay of his own. It is hardly Box Brown's book.

Fearful of capture because of the Fugitive Slave Act of 1850, Brown was forced to flee to England soon after his arrival in the North. In England, he, or someone under his direction, edited Stearns' overblown rhetoric out of the narrative, and a new version was issued in Manchester in 1851. The excision of Sterns' words and rhetoric is clear evidence of the kinds of restrictions ex-slaves faced under the control of their best anti-slavery white friends. Unable to read or write and with little access to printers or publishers, Box Brown was not free from saying what other people wanted him to say. Only in England did he experience the freedom to express himself in his own way. The Manchester editon is obviously closer to Brown's own telling of his own story, but it has never been published in the United States—until now.

The differences between the two books are clear from their titles. The American title is *Narrative of Henry Box Brown who Escaped from Slavery Enclosed in a Box 3 Feet Long and 2 Wide Written from a Statement of Facts Made by Himself. With Remarks upon the Remedy for*

Slavery. By Charles Stearns. The This book, a reprinting of Brown's Manchester version, is simply entitled *Narrative of the Life of Henry Box Brown, Written by Himself* and is twenty-three pages shorter. The real difference is that this version is told in Brown's own voice.

In their original published forms, both these books are scarce. Philip McBlain, the leading dealer in rare African-American books, reports that he has never seen a copy of the American edition. The New York book dealer Glen Horowitz did offer one for sale in 1996 at $5,500. It does exist in major research libraries, however, and there were several reprints in the late 1960s, but now even these have disappeared. A dozen copies of this 1851 Manchester edition are in American libraries.

A second English edition came out in Bilston in 1852, but the stereotyped text is the same as this volume. The Bilston reprint indicates the book's popularity in the United Kingdom, where Brown became a feature on the abolitionist lecture circuit, as he had been in the United States. Currently, there is only one known copy of the 1852 edition in the United States.

Brown's Life in Slavery

Box Brown's birthdate, like that of all slaves, is uncertain, but we know he was born on a plantation in Louisa County, Virginia, near the capital city of Richmond, sometime around 1815. The first half of the nineteenth century through which he lived was a momentous period for a nation struggling with the crisis of slavery. The very existence of the United States as a federal union was at stake, first when the moralistic New England abolitionists cried, "No union with slaveholders," then when the white South used states' rights as a rationalization to protect the slave system.

Brown lived through a time of increasing national polarization. In the years before he became a fugitive, the South toughened its position, particularly as it saw the western territories as potential ground for the addition of slave states. In 1816, the American Colonization Society was formed to eliminate the "danger" of free Negroes in a slave society by shipping them to Africa. In the 1830s, black literacy was forbidden by law in many states. In 1836, a gag rule forbade even the introduction of anti-slavery legislation in the U.S. Congress. When pro-slavery Missouri applied for statehood in 1818, Thomas Jefferson perceptively called it "a firebell in the night," an alarm and a warning that an inevitable conflagration lay ahead.

African Americans also strengthened their own resolve during Brown's lifetime. In 1827, the first black newspaper, *Freedom's Journal*, appeared in New York with the statement, "Too long have others spoken for us." Two years later, David Walker published in Boston his radical *Appeal*, calling for slave revolt. In 1831 Nat Turner in Virginia led the slaves' most successful rebellion. The famous *L'Amistad* mutiny was in 1839, and in 1843 Sojourner Truth became an anti-slavery activist. Personal escapes that came to national attention increased: Frederick Douglass in 1838, William and Ellen Craft in 1848, and Harriet Tubman just four months after Box Brown, in 1849.

Brown's Extraordinary Escape

The whole purpose of Brown's *Narrative* was, and continues to be, the creation of a medium for him to tell his own story. He describes his family and childhood, his work in a tobacco factory, and the heart-breaking account of the sale of his wife and children, which meant their forced separation. It was then that this law-abiding man decided to escape, and "the idea suddenly flashed upon my mind of shutting myself up in a box and getting myself conveyed as dry goods to a free State."

What did the slaves themselves, particularly the vast majority who were the plantation field hands, say was the worst aspect of bondage? It was not the whippings, the labor of sixteen-hour workdays, the food minimized to survival levels, the special clothing woven from mill-floor scraps. Their deepest anxiety and greatest suffering came from the arbitrary breaking up of their families, husbands from wives, parents from children, children from each other. This severance and sundering created an emotional death that left scars deeper than the lash marks on their backs.

Brown's five-foot, eight-inch, 200-pound body was fitted into a baize-lined container sealed by five hickory loops, marked "THIS SIDE UP WITH CARE," and mailed to William H. Johnson, an abolitionist sympathizer on Philadelphia's Arch Street. The city's Anti-Slavery Committee sent for the box, and it was brought to their office at 107 N. 5th Street on March 30, 1849. Nervous abolitionists opened the box, Henry Brown calmly emerged, said, "How do you do, gentlemen?" and promptly fainted.

After a glass of water, a disheveled Brown regained his aplomb and proceeded to sing the Fortieth Psalm. Provided with money and clothes, Brown stayed with abolitionists James and Lucretia Mott, and then was sent to Boston and New Bedford. Brown's imaginative escape immediately caught public attention. He became an instant celebrity, a status he discovered he liked and learned to exploit. He went on the abolitionist lecture circuit, singing his songs and telling his story.

Sentiment against slavery was rising in the North, largely because a national government dominated by pro-slavery southerners was pushing its agenda. Brown, and others, found increasingly sympathetic audiences. Northern whites were particularly attracted to fugitive slaves who could describe from their own experiences what slavery was really like. They were fascinated by Brown, in part, of course, because of his successful but dangerous escape. He stayed on tour until the early fall of 1850.

Legal Ramifications

Back in Virginia, meanwhile, the seriousness of Brown's escape was dramatized by the arrest of Samuel A. Smith, the white man who facilitated Brown's flight by packing him into his famous box. Smith was convicted in October 1849 for boxing up two more potential escapees, Alfred and Sawney, who were discovered and captured. Smith was refused witnesses, and spent five summer months chained in a cell five feet by eight feet, not unlike the restrained enclosure of his friend Brown. In prison, Smith survived five stab wounds, reportedly inflicted by a hired assassin. Like St. Paul, however, Smith converted his jailer—who petitioned the governor of Virginia for Smith's release. The governor refused, and Smith was not set free until June 18, 1856.

James Caesar Anthony Smith, the free black who helped Samuel Smith ship Brown to Philadelphia, was also arrested and tried. He allegedly introduced Alfred and Sawney to Samuel Smith, and he was therefore charged as an accomplice in the conspiracy to assist their escape. J.C.A. Smith also allegedly outfitted escape trunks that had been constructed by John Mattauer, a black carpenter. Smith admitted having helped slaves escape since 1826. Interestingly, while the white Samuel Smith was convicted, the black J.C.A. Smith was released, perhaps because a lawyer who charged $900 argued his case.

Immediately following his release, Samuel A. Smith left the South for Philadelphia, the same destination as Brown. Well aware of his role in Brown's escape as well as Smith's own personal suffering, Philadelphia's African-

American community held a mass meeting on his behalf at the Israel Church on July 1, 1856. After hearing Smith quietly recount his experience in prison, the meeting passed this resolution:

> We the colored citizens of Philadelphia, have among us Samuel A. Smith, who was incarcerated over seven years in Richmond Penitentiary, for doing an act that was honorable to his feelings and his sense of justice and humanity, therefore.
>
> Resolved, That we welcome him to this city as a martyr to the cause of Freedom.
>
> Resolved, That we heartily tender him our gratitude for the good he has done to our suffering race.

Resistance, Escape, and the Underground Railroad

Although history has long recognized white abolitionists, it has largely ignored the anti-slavery struggle of African Americans, even though it was the blacks themselves who were the real abolitionists. The people who were against slavery were, after all, the slaves. There were 3,204,313 slaves in the United States in 1850, owned by 347,725 white families. Slave resistance to bondage started at the plantation itself: slowed-down work, theft, broken tools, stable doors left open, crops damaged, dissembling, feigned illnesses. There was a second level: burned barns and poisoned soup. And a third: armed rebellion. At least 250 slave revolts in the United States have been documented, and recent research on the Atlantic slave trade documents another 250 aboard ship.

In the North, free blacks supported their brothers and sisters in chains. Most opposed the American Colonization Society, and strengthened their resolve to achieve black freedom in this country. African Americans organized themselves against slavery, petitioned, founded newspapers, held mass meetings, and even urged slave rebellion. There were over fifty black anti-slavery societies by 1830, all before William Lloyd Garrison formed the American Anti-Slavery Society in 1833. Garrison's famous *Liberator* newspaper was subsidized and subscribed to by people of color.

The major resistance to slavery, however, was escape, what Frederick Douglass called "praying with your feet." With his unique variation, this was the means Box Brown chose to free himself. Running away was by definition a secret and dangerous undertaking, not only illegal, but with high prices to pay by those who were captured. As a result, many aspects and elements of the process are not now fully known.

Following the North Star

Many runaways followed the North Star to the free states and Canada, but a large number, almost entirely undocumented, escaped to Mexico, where they disappeared into the population. The estimate is that several thousand slaves became fugitives from the South's "peculiar institution" each year during the first half of the nineteenth century.

It was not death, but life, not heaven, but Canada that was the encoded message of the slave song:

> No more auction block for me,
> No more, no more.
> No more auction block for me,
> Many thousand gone.

While many fugitives made their way on their own, others followed the Underground Railroad, a loose network of clandestine escape routes. There were signals, disguises, passwords, safe houses, and guides or "conductors." With a price on her head, Harriet Tubman made repeated trips below the Mason-Dixon line to bring out men, women, and children. Fugitives traveled by boat and wagon, but mostly by foot, often walking at night and hiding during the day, but always heading North. Since slaves were legally defined as property, escape was actually a curious form of the slaves' stealing themselves.

We are just now discovering some of the hidden aspects of escape. African-American-made quilts, for example, innocently airing in a cabin window, were sometimes disguised maps, and could contain coded messages about dangers and directions. It is now well-known that the slave songs or Negro Spirituals are full of allusions to escape as well as ways of communicating within the black community without white people understanding what was being said. In these songs, for example, Canaan is Canada; the Jordan is the Ohio River (the dividing line between the slave and free states); and the many references to travel (shoes, wheels, chariots, trains) are all about running away. . . .

Brown's New Life

Success as a speaker and singer performing on the antislavery circuit not only agreed with Brown, it encouraged his abilities as an entrepreneur. The imagination that led him in the first place to his box now blossomed into an idea for a massive and spectacular panorama, a pictorial representation exhibited with changing scenes. A panorama as such was not an original idea of Brown's, but he grasped its potential significance both as a way to communicate the story of slavery through revealing comprehensible images, as well as to appeal to a public always receptive to something new and different.

On February 1, 1850, Brown wrote Gerrit Smith, the wealthy white abolitionist, and asked for a loan of $150 to pay for his panorama. Brown engaged Josiah Wolcott to design and paint it, perhaps with the assistance of other artists. Wolcott was a white painter of portraits and of New England natural scenes in the Hudson River School style. One of his better known works is of Brook Farm, the utopian community in West Roxbury, Massachusetts. Brown's panorama was entitled *The Mirror of Slavery*. It is now lost, but it certainly consisted of many thousands of square feet of canvas.

Brown made a second inspired choice in recruiting Benjamin F. Roberts to prepare an accompanying text and lecture, "The Condition of the Colored People in the United States." Roberts was an African-American Boston printer who, the year before, had filed a suit for the integration of Boston's public schools on behalf of his daughter Sarah, but the state Supreme Court ruled in favor of the city. Roberts also represented "A Committee of Colored Gentlemen" who had reissued in 1844 R.B. Lewis's *Light and Truth*, one of the first histories of people of color by an African American.

The Mirror of Slavery opened to the public on April 19, 1850, in Washington Hall on Boston's Bromfield Street. Admission was twenty-five cents for adults, with children at half-price. The panorama was exhibited for several months, and then it traveled to other New England towns in a tour coordinated by Roberts. When Brown fled the country in September, he managed to transport *The Mirror of Slavery* to England. Now accompanied by J.C.A. Smith, Brown put *The Mirror of Slavery* back on the road until the men split up and each went his separate way.

Images of Black History

The Mirror of Slavery was not only a presentation by people of color, it portrayed images and views of American history as people of color perceived that history. The panorama of some fifty pictures opened with the beginning of it all, *The African Slave Trade*, the centuries old human commerce that had devastated Africa and corrupted America. The second and third images, *The Nubian Family in Freedom* and *The Seizure of Slaves*, revealed the destruction of the Old World; they were followed by *The Nubian Family at Auction* and *Modes of Confinement and Punishment* that revealed the depravity of the New World.

Brown aptly alternated traditional American scenic views, like *View of Richmond, Va.* with such scenes as *Whipping Post and Gallows at Richmond, Va.* He did the same with *Washington's Tomb at Mount Vernon* and *Slave Prisons at Washington.* This interspersion threw into question every conventional idea of the American landscape. . . . Brown's . . . picture of America transformed sentimental representations into an honest reality most white Americans had never seen. Not to minimize his own historical role, Brown included two images of his own escape.

Flight to England

The Compromise of 1850 was another futile attempt to hold together an America deeply fractured over the issue of slavery. For African Americans and their white abolitionist friends, the most objectionable feature of the Compromise was its strengthened Fugitive Slave Act. Now federal law required free people in the North to aid in the capture and return of black runaways. The law was often met with noncompliance and even resistance. On August 30, 1850, Henry Box Brown narrowly escaped capture by slave agents in Providence, Rhode Island. So did his tour companion, J.C.A. Smith, even though he was a freeborn Negro.

Both men fled to England, arriving in Liverpool in late October. Brown lectured, sold lithographs of himself, and sang spirituals, anti-slavery songs, and hymns to raise money for the shipment of his panorama. With *The Mirror of Slavery* Brown and Smith toured the north of England in the winter and spring of 1850–1851. Brown's showmanship developed even further, and he had himself shipped, theatrically, in his famous box from Bradford to Leeds.

Friction, probably over money, developed between Brown and Smith, and Brown officially dissolved their partnership on July 25, 1851. Now both men traveled the U.K. lecture circuit, each with his own panorama. We next get a picture of a new and different Brown, but it is hardly an unbiased view since it comes from the spurned J.C.A. Smith. On August 6 from Manchester, Smith wrote Gerrit Smith to complain about Brown's breaking up their partnership and allegedly taking the money.

"Brown has behaved very bad sense he have been here," Smith asserted, citing Brown's drinking, smoking, gambling, swearing, and said he "do many other things too Bad—to think off." What could be too bad to think of? "He have got it to his head to get a wife or something *worst.*" Smith claimed Brown could have purchased his enslaved wife and children from their American bondage, but that he was apparently being seduced into the fast life of England. What was the evidence?

Smith said Brown was drinking "Rasbury wine, pop, pepermint, Sampson, ginger Beer, gingerale, Blackbeer . . . and many other things of that nature," although he admitted none of these beverages was actually alcoholic. Brown was also "smoking pipe, segars, and chewing tobacco, takin' snuff," as well as swearing. The gambling consisted of "playing doman noes-dice, drafts, and Begertels." These may seem like innocent pastimes, but they were intended to discredit Brown by being reported to the pietistic and moralistic white American abolitionist community.

What happened to Brown is as yet unknown. Various unsubstantiated rumors have him adding minstrelsy to his performance, marrying an Englishwoman, and disappearing into Wales. No one has made a concerted effort to track Brown at this point, but there must be newspapers and civic records that could complete his story. Brown began and spent most of his life in anonymity, and, at least so far as we now know, ended it the same way. . . .

Brown's life and work personify several of the interconnected themes integral to African-American experience and culture. First, he reinvents himself. Once a slave, he becomes free; once a factory worker, he becomes an abolitionist lecturer, writer, and performer; once a nonentity, he becomes somebody. He even changes his name to mark the defining event in his life and signify his new identity. In Britain, if his critic is to be believed, he transposes himself still further, from a humble, religious abolitionist to something of a worldly dandy.

Second, Brown improvises, personally incorporating the essence of black speech, style, and music. His box is an original method of self-liberation. . . . Brown's performance keeps adding new riffs, from songs and a massive panorama, to perhaps even elements of minstrelsy. The reinvented Brown finds that the black cultural tradition of improvisation is, in truth, his way to meet, live, and prevail in his new life.

Literary critic Houston A. Baker points out that every African American serves a prison sentence—enslaved on plantations, segregated into ghettos, incarcerated in prisons and housing projects, trapped in ignorance and poverty, constrained in a box of one kind or another. It is precisely this imprisonment Henry Box Brown confronts, challenges, and defeats. Brown's final word and continuing message is that he used confinement to achieve his liberation.

Sojourner Truth

Elizabeth Shafer

At nearly six feet tall, Sojourner Truth was literally a towering figure in the abolitionist and women's rights movements. Born a slave named Isabella Baumfree in 1797 in Ulster County, New York, as an adult she came to be known as Sojourner Truth, preacher, antislavery activist, and feminist. The following biographical sketch explains how Truth's new name reflected her sense of her life's mission: as a traveler, even a pilgrim, for truth. For Sojourner, "truth" could be achieved only through emancipation, woman suffrage, and Christian love. But Elizabeth Shafer points out that Truth was more than a visionary. Truth was also a fighter who sought practical (if sometimes unorthodox) solutions to real-world problems: newly free, she won a successful lawsuit to emancipate her son; years later, she responded to a white man's challenge of her gender by publicly baring her breasts.

   Elizabeth Shafer is author of "Sojourner Truth: A Self-Made Woman," as well as writer of a sourcebook for teaching J.K. Rowlings's *Harry Potter* books.

🔸 🔸 🔸

She was over 6 feet tall, rawboned, black, and—for the first forty years of her life—a slave. The next forty-six years she spent becoming, as she said, "a self-made woman."

Sojourner Truth was a powerful and eloquent speaker against slavery and for women's rights, lecturing in twenty-one states and the District of Columbia from 1843 until 1878, when she was 81. She was a friend and coworker of the great names among the abolitionists and fighters for women's rights. She was a guest of Harriet Beecher Stowe, who celebrated her as "The Libyan Sibyl" in *The Atlantic Monthly*; and she was received at the White House by Abraham Lincoln.

Those who heard her speak and sing in her deep, strong voice never forgot her nor her shrewd wit, simple wisdom, and droll humor. Mrs. Stowe wrote of the "power and sweetness in that great warm soul and that vigorous frame," adding, "I do not recall ever to have been conversant with anyone who had more of that silent and subtle power which we call personal presence than this woman." From the sister of the famous preacher and spellbinder, Henry Ward Beecher, this was the ultimate compliment.

Isabella's Childhood

She was born in 1797 in Ulster County, New York, the twelfth child of Bomefree [or Baumfree] and Mama Bett, slaves of a Dutchman, Charles Hardenbergh. (New York and New Jersey were the last of the northern states to keep slaves; the other states had abolished slavery following the Revolution.) When Sojourner was about 11, Hardenbergh died, and "Isabella," as she was then called, was sold at an auction of "slaves, horses, and other cattle" to a Yankee storekeeper, John Nealy. Nealy paid a hundred dollars for the gawky child and a herd of sheep.

Years later she was to say, "Now the war begun." For Isabella spoke only Low Dutch, and the Nealys spoke only English. When her father learned how they beat her, he begged a local tavernkeeper to buy her. She lived eighteen months with the Scrivers, working in the house and in the fields and serving customers in the tavern. She was 13 now, and already 6 feet tall.

She was happy those brief months, but in 1810 John J. Dumont of nearby New Paltz bought her for $300. (As a sturdy young woman, her value was going up.) Dumont was a large slaveholder by New York standards, keeping ten slaves. They all lived in a large room behind the kitchen called the slave kitchen.

Marriage and Motherhood

Isabella was a good worker—too good in the opinion of her fellow slaves, who called her "white man's nigger." She fell in love with "Catlin's Robert," as slaves were identified in those days. But Robert's master beat him terribly and forced him to marry one of the Catlin slaves. Isabella, in turn, was married to old Thomas, one of Dumont's slaves. They were to have five children.

While she was chiefly a house slave for Mrs. Dumont, she also worked in the fields. She would put her latest baby in a basket, tie a rope to the handles, and suspend it in a tree, where a small child was set to swinging it.

Meanwhile, New York State had passed a new law. All slaves born before July 4, 1799, were to be freed on July 4, 1827. All slaves younger than 28 were "free"—but had to work as unpaid servants until the boys were 28, the girls 25. Because she was such a faithful worker, Dumont promised Isabella he would free her a year early. But in the summer of 1826, he refused to fulfill his promise.

Isabella remembered the Quaker, Levi Rowe, who had said to her once, years before, "Thou should not be a slave." She took her youngest child, Sophia, leaving the others at Dumont's with Thomas, and walked to Rowe's farm.

Rowe was dying, but he sent her on to Mr. and Mrs. Isaac S. Van Wagener. When Dumont followed, demanding his property, the Van Wageners agreed to buy Isabella's services for the rest of the year for twenty dollars, and the child's services until she was 25 for five dollars. However, they instructed Isabella not to call them "master" and "mistress," and she was treated as a paid servant.

A Message from God

Once she became homesick and almost agreed to accompany Dumont back to his farm, but as she was heading for the gate she heard a voice: "Not another step!" She quickly returned to her room, where she prayed for strength. Her mother had long ago taught her the Lord's prayer in Low Dutch, and had told her solemnly, "There is a God, who hears and sees you." It was at this crisis in her life that Isabella discovered Jesus. But she was afraid, she said afterwards, that the whites would discover that Jesus was her friend and take him from her as they had taken everything else, so she kept her new friend a secret.

There was a small island in a nearby stream. Here she wove a wall of willows and conducted private talks with God and Jesus. She was to continue this very personal dialog for the rest of her life.

On "freedom day," July 4, 1827, Isaac and Maria Van Wagener conducted a small private ceremony, reading from the Bible. Maria kissed Isabella on the cheek. "Take thy Sophia, too, into freedom," she said, handing her the child. They agreed upon wages for her labor, and Isabella and the child lived with them for another two years.

Her son, Peter, had disappeared, and Isabella finally learned that Dumont had sold the boy to a family whose daughter had taken Peter south to Alabama. This meant, of course, that he would never be free.

When Isabella spoke to Mrs. Dumont about Peter, the woman jeered at her. Isabella drew herself to her full height and cried in her deep voice, "I'll have my child again!" She was to recall afterwards, "When I spoke to my mistress that way, I felt so tall within. I felt as if the power of a nation was within me."

Isabella Appeals to the Law

An abolitionist advised her to go to a certain Quaker for help. She arrived at night, and was given a room of her own with a tall poster bed. She remembered later, "I was scared when she left me alone with that great white bed. I had never been in a real bed in my life. It never came into my mind she could mean me to sleep on it. So I just camped under it, and I slept pretty well there on the floor."

Next morning, she took her case to the grand jury at Kingston. This was the first of many battles she was to undertake and win. The woman who was to become Sojourner Truth believed in the power of the law and used it effectively for herself and her people.

Peter was returned to her, and the two went to New York City in 1829. But the boy fell into bad company and she was forced to send him to sea. He sent her several letters, saying he had received none of her. Then he stopped writing; she never heard from him again.

The Birth of "Sojourner"

While in New York she learned English, which she always spoke with a heavy Dutch accent, and worked as a domestic for various families and for a religious group called The Kingdom. But in 1843, she had a vision. She took her clothes, some bread and cheese, and twenty-five cents for the ferry to Brooklyn. "I am no longer Isabella," she said. "I am Sojourner." But Sojourner what? She gave the matter some thought. Remembering that a slave always took the name of her master, she said, "Oh, God, thou art my last master, and thy name is Truth, so shall Truth be my abiding name until I die."

And so, at 46, Sojourner Truth was born.

The year 1843 was a time of great religious revival. Reform was in the air. Abolitionists were calling for an end to slavery. Talk of women's rights would culminate in the first Women's Rights Convention at Seneca, New York, in 1848. Men and women were setting up religious communities. Camp meetings were held everywhere.

Truth's Public Life Begins

In her wanderings, Sojourner came upon her first camp meeting. She began to speak and sing at many such gatherings. Later, she advertised and conducted meetings of her own. Olive Gilbert, who was the first to help Sojourner put her story into print (*Narrative of Sojourner Truth: A Northern Slave*, 1850) commented, "All who have ever heard her sing . . . will probably remember it as long as they remember her."

At one such camp meeting, a group of rowdies threatened to disrupt the proceedings. Sojourner walked to one side, on a little knoll, and began to sing. The rowdies gathered around her, begging her to sing some more, and became quiet. They even laughed appreciatively when she told them, "Well, there are two congregations on this ground. It is written that the sheep shall be separated from the goats. The other preachers have the sheep, I have the goats. I have a few sheep among my goats, but they are very ragged." Both meetings went on without incident after that.

Abolition and Women's Rights

She met all the great figures of the abolition movement: Samuel Hill, Wendell Phillips, Parker Pillsbury, Frederick Douglass, and William Lloyd Garrison.

These men also worked with women in organizing the first women's rights convention. Sojourner knew Lucretia Mott, Susan B. Anthony. Elizabeth Cady Stanton, and Lucy Stone. She was the only black delegate to the Worcester, Massachusetts, women's rights convention in 1850. Men jeered, newspapers called it the Hen Convention, and one minister even threatened to expel from his congregation any member daring to attend.

It was at this convention that Sojourner, ever the militant, asked, "If women want any rights more'n they've got, why don't they just take 'em and not be talking about it?"

She was a faithful fighter for all women's rights, but she drew the line at the current fad of wearing "bloomers." Recalling her days as a slave who got only a single length of cloth to cover her long frame and so had to stitch up the legs for modesty, she declared, "Tell *you*, I had enough of bloomers in them days!"

Growing Fame

With the passage of the Fugitive Slave Act in 1850, the abolitionists redoubled their activities. Sojourner was invited to join them on their speaking tours.

She often traveled alone, in a borrowed buggy loaded with copies of her book, song sheets of her own composing, and copies of her photograph ("I sell the shadow to support the substance.") She would give the horse its head, saying, "God, you drive." It always seemed to turn out right. She would stop at a crossroads or in a village square, unfold the freedom banner which the Akron, Ohio, women's rights convention had given her, and speak and sing.

One of her own songs, eleven stanzas long, began:

I am pleading for my people—
A poor, down-trodden race,

Who dwell in freedom's boasted land
With no abiding place.
I am pleading that my people
May have their rights restored,
For they have long been toiling
And yet have no reward.

Uncle Tom's Cabin had received instant acclaim in 1852, and, wanting to meet the author, Sojourner appeared at Harriet Beecher Stowe's home in Andover, Massachusetts. Harriet was so taken with her visitor that she invited her to stay for several days. "An audience was what she wanted," Harriet was to write later. "It mattered not whether high or low, learned or ignorant. She had things to say, and was ready to say them at all times, and to anyone."

Sojourner Proves Her Gender

In 1857 the *Dred Scott* decision ruled that a slave could not be a citizen, and that Congress had no power to exclude slavery from the western territories. This precipitated new abolitionist activity. Sojourner went into Indiana with Parker Pillsbury. It was during this speaking tour that a hostile doctor rose and demanded that she show her breasts to a group of women from the audience. He said, "Your voice is not the voice of a woman, it is the voice of a man, and we believe you are a man."

Silently, Sojourner Truth, now 60, undid her Quaker kerchief and opened her dress, displaying her breasts to the whole congregation. "It is not my shame but yours that I do this," she said.

On the Eve of War

Events began moving more swiftly now. In 1859, John Brown raided Harpers Ferry. In 1860, Lincoln was elected President. And by April 1861, Fort Sumter had been fired upon.

Josephine Griffing of Ohio asked Sojourner to accompany her on an anti-slavery lecture tour into Indiana, where Copperheads (pro-slavery forces) controlled the legislature. This was a dangerous undertaking, but Sojourner agreed at once. Two miles across the Ohio-Indiana border, she was arrested. Josephine got a court order for her release. Hecklers broke up their first meeting and they were taken into protective custody by a member of the Union home guard, who escorted them to Angola. Here, the Copperheads threatened to burn the building where Sojourner was to speak.

"Then I will speak upon the ashes," she said firmly.

The women of the town dressed her in a red, white, and blue shawl with a sash and apron to match. She wore a cap with a star, and a star on each shoulder. Sojourner remembered:

> When we were ready to go, they put me into a large, beautiful carriage with the captain and other gentlemen, all of whom were armed. The soldiers walked by our side and a long procession followed. As we neared the court house, looking out of the window I saw that the building was surrounded by a great crowd. I felt as I was going against the Philistines and I prayed the Lord to deliver me out of their hands. But when the rebels saw such a mighty army coming, they fled, and by the time we arrived they were scattered over the fields, looking like a flock of frightened crows, and not one was left but a small boy, who sat upon the fence, crying, "Nigger, nigger!"

The procession marched into the court house, everyone sang, and she spoke without interruption.

The tour was a triumph, but it exhausted her. She was ill for some time, and there were rumors she was dead. But the Emancipation Proclamation of January 1, 1863, heartened her; she declared that she must get well.

Slowly, over the years, she had been gathering her family about her in Battle Creek, Michigan—her daughters and grandsons Sammy and James, who sometimes acted as escorts on her journeys. When she was not lecturing, she earned her living as she always did, cooking, cleaning house, doing laundry, and caring for the sick.

Wartime Activism
Grandson James Caldwell had joined the Union Army now that they were accepting Negroes. At Thanksgiving in 1863, Sojourner visited the 1st Michigan Colored Infantry at Detroit, taking them donations of good things to eat. She taught them to sing her latest song, to the tune of *John Brown's Body*:

> We are the valiant soldiers who've 'listed for
>   the war;
> We are fighting for the Union, we are fighting
>   for the law;
> We can shoot a rebel farther than a white man
>   ever saw.
> As we go marching on. . . .

From Detroit, she went to New York, speaking to Henry Ward Beecher's Brooklyn congregation at Plymouth Church. And on October 29, 1864, she met Abraham Lincoln at the White House. The President signed her "Book of Life," an autograph book containing the signatures of many of the most famous people of her time.

She found plenty to do in Washington. She spoke to the Colored Soldiers' Aid Society. She worked at Arlington Heights, Virginia as a counselor for the National Freedmen's Relief Association, and that autumn she was asked to help the surgeon in charge of the Freedmen's Hospital to "promote order, cleanliness, industry, and virtue among the patients."

Continuing the Fight
Before the war, the streetcars in Washington had been segregated. After Lincoln signed a law outlawing dis-

crimination in Washington public transportation, many conductors simply refused to stop for black passengers. One day Sojourner Truth stood in the middle of the street and shouted three times at the top of her lungs, "I WANT TO RIDE!" She nearly panicked the horses, but she managed to get on, then refused to stand on the platform behind the horses, "I am a passenger and shall sit with the other passengers."

In a later incident, an irate conductor slammed her against the door, pushing her shoulder out of joint. Again, she went to court. The Freedmen's Bureau lawyer sued the company, the conductor lost his job, and from then on blacks rode the Washington streetcars.

In 1867, escorted by grandson Sammy, she traveled through western New York, seeking jobs for freed slaves. Journalist Theodore Tilton asked permission to write her life story. She replied, "I am not ready to be writ up yet, for I have still lots to accomplish." And in 1870 she set out on "the last great mission of her life"— petitioning Congress for free land for the former slaves. But Senator Charles Sumner, who had worked for passage of the bill, died. Then grandson Sammy fell ill and died. Sojourner herself suffered a stroke and a lengthy illness. The petition for free land failed, one of the few failures in her long and productive life.

Last Years

In the nation's centennial year, she celebrated her eightieth birthday. Her paralysis had disappeared, her hair began to grow in black instead of its former gray, and as writers of the period commented, her deep voice had lost none of its power. When she was 81, she spoke in thirty-six different towns in her home state of Michigan. And in July of that year, she was one of three Michigan delegates to the 30th anniversary meeting of the Women's Rights Convention.

While her dream of free land had not been realized, she was to see 60,000 freedmen take up homesteads in Kansas by the end of 1879.

Sojourner Truth died at her home in Battle Creek on November 26, 1883, with her family around her. She was buried at Oak Hill Cemetery. Many of her early friends were dead or too old to attend the services, but Frederick Douglass sent a message, as did Wendell Phillips. A thousand friends and neighbors filed past her coffin. Among the floral offerings was a great sheaf of ripened wheat from the freedmen of Kansas.

Once when a friend had asked, "But Sojourner, what if there is no heaven?" she had replied, "What will I say if I don't get there? Why, I'll say, 'Bless the Lord! I had a good time thinking I would!'"

A Newspaper Account of the Turner Rebellion

Richmond Enquirer

The following selection is an excerpt from a Richmond newspaper's account of the Nat Turner insurrection published on August 30, 1831, less than two weeks after the rebellion broke out and two months before its leader was apprehended. Perhaps unsurprisingly given the horrific attacks on the white victims, the writer characterizes Turner and his followers as monsters and animals. Nonetheless, it is significant to note the article's implication that Turner's actions were spawned by his literacy and his religious education. Many slave states had strict laws forbidding teaching slaves to read and write lest abolitionist literature reach and sway them to defy their masters. Frederick Douglass secretly learned to read and write from his owner's wife. As for Christian education, slaveholders had more ambivalent views. Although Christianity exalted the submissiveness, forbearance, and obedience that masters wished to instill in their slaves, it also claimed that Jesus favored the meek and the poor, and it urged all men to love their neighbors as themselves. In short, the Christianity endorsed by slave interests was a highly selective version, and

"Nat Turner's Rebellion," *Richmond Enquirer*, August 30, 1831

Turner's violent fanaticism seemed to exemplify the need for greater control and vigilance where slaves' spiritual instruction was concerned.

Interestingly as well, the writer seems to take pains to reassure readers that most slaves were eager to assist the militia in quelling the rebellion and capturing the miscreants. The tone of the article suggests a dual, perhaps contradictory purpose: both to assure readers that the insurrection, however bloody, was an aberration, and to subtly suggest its causes (i.e., literacy and religion) that must be addressed to prevent future rebellions.

*   *   *

So much curiosity has been excited in the state, and so much exaggeration will go abroad, that we have determined to devote a great portion of this day's paper to the strange events in the county of Southampton. . . . What strikes us as the most remarkable thing in this matter is the horrible ferocity of these monsters. They remind one of a parcel of blood-thirsty wolves rushing down from the Alps; or rather like a former incursion of the Indians upon the white settlements. Nothing is spared; neither age nor sex is respected—the helplessness of women and children pleads in vain for mercy. The danger is thought to be over—but prudence still demands precaution. The lower country should be on the alert.—The case of Nat Turner warns us. No black man ought to be permitted to turn a Preacher through the country. The law must be enforced or the tragedy of Southampton appeals to us in vain.

Extract of a letter from Jerusalem, Va., 24th August, 3 o'clock—The oldest inhabitants of our county have never experienced such a distressing time, as we have had since Sunday night last. The negroes, about fifteen miles from this place, have massacred from 50 to 75 women and children, and some 8 or 10 men. Every house, room and corner in this place is full of women and children, driven from home, who had to take the woods, until they could get to this place. We are worn out with fatigue.

Turner and His Followers

A fanatic preacher by the name of Nat Turner (Gen. Nat Turner) who had been taught to read and write, and permitted to go about preaching in the country, was at the bottom of this infernal brigandage. He was artful, impudent and vindicative, without any cause or provocation, that could be assigned.—He was the slave of Mr. Travis. He and another slave of Mr. T. a young fellow, by the name of Moore, were two of the leaders. Three or four others were first concerned and most active.—They had 15 others to join them. And by importunity or threats they prevailed upon about 20 others to cooperate in the scheme of massacre. We cannot say how long they were organizing themselves—but they turned out on last Monday early (the 22d) upon their nefarious expedition. . . . They were mounted to the number of 40 or 50; and with knives and axes—knocking on the head, or cutting the throats of their victims. They had few firearms among them—and scarcely one, if one, was fit for use. . . . But as they went from house to house, they drank ardent spirits—and it is supposed, that in consequence of their being intoxicated,—or from mere fatigue, they paused in their murderous career about 12 o'clock on Monday.

The Victims

A fact or two, before we continue our narrative. These wretches are now estimated to have committed sixty-one murders! Not a white person escaped at all the houses they visited except two. One was a little child at Mrs. Waller's, about 7 or 8 years of age, who had sagacity enough to creep up a chimney; and the other was Mrs. Barrow, whose husband was murdered in his cotton patch, though he had received some notice in the course of the morning of the murderous deeds that were going on; but placed no confidence in the story and fell victim to his incredulty. His wife hid herself between weather-boarding, and the unplastered lathing, and escaped, the wretches not taking time to hunt her out. It was believed that one of the brigands had taken up a spit against Mr. Barrow, because he had refused him one of his female slaves for a wife.

Early on Tuesday morning, they attempted to renew their bloody work. They made an attack upon Mr. Blunt, a gentleman who was very unwell with the gout, and who instead of flying determined to brave them out. He had several pieces of firearms, perhaps seven or eight, and he put them into the hands of his own slaves, who nobly and gallantly stood by him. They repelled the brigands—killed one, wounded and took prisoner (Gen. Moore), and we believe took a third who was not wounded at all. . . .

Pursuit of the Culprits

The militia of Southampton had been most active in ferreting out the fugitives from their hiding places. . . . But it deserves to be said to the credit of many of the slaves whom gratitude had bound to their masters, that they had manifested the greatest alacrity in detecting and apprehending many of the brigands. They had brought in several and a fine spirit had been shown in many of the plantations of confidence on the part of the masters, and gratitude on that of the slaves. It is said that from 40 to 50 blacks were in jail—some of whom were known to be concerned with the murders, and others suspected. The courts will discriminate the innocent from the guilty.

It is believed that all the brigands were slaves—and most, if not all these, the property of kind and indulgent masters. It is not known that any of them had been the runaways of the swamps and only one of them was a free man of color. He had afterwards returned to his own house, and a party sent there to apprehend him. He was accidently seen concealed in his yard and shot. . . .

Nat, the ringleader, who calls himself General, pretends to be a Baptist preacher's great enthusiasts—declares to his comrades that he is commissioned by Jesus Christ, and proceeds under his inspired directions—that the late singular appearance of the sun was the sign for him, etc., etc., is among the number not yet taken. The story of his having been killed at the bridge, and of two engagements there, is ungrounded. It is believed he cannot escape.

The General [i.e., General Broadnax, the militia commander in Greensville County] is convinced, from various sources of information, that there existed no general concert among the slaves.—Circumstances impossible to have been feigned, demonstrate the entire ignorance on the subject of all the slaves in the counties around Southampton, among whom he has never known more perfect order and quiet to prevail.

Equality for Blacks, Equality for Women

Sojourner Truth

Although the abolitionist and woman suffrage movements were both key aspects of the larger nineteenth-century reform movement that took root in America, the end of the Civil War brought a renewed interest in the debate over voting rights. The annual meeting of the American Equal Rights Association convened, for the first time, in New York City in May 1867, its expressed goal "to secure Equal Rights to all American Citizens, especially the Right of Suffrage, irrespective of race, color or sex." Subject to sometimes heated argument was the matter of whether women's right to vote should be linked with the suffrage of black men. Some reformers felt that change was best effected in increments, believing that achieving the vote for black males should take precedence. Others, such as Elizabeth Cady Stanton, Lucretia Mott, and Henry Ward Beecher, insisted that suffrage rights should apply to all citizens regardless of race *or* gender. Sojourner Truth, no stranger to either movement, addressed the meeting to express her strong support for women's civil rights along with those of blacks. Truth claims that universal suffrage was a

Sojourner Truth, address to the First Annual Meeting of the American Equal Rights Association, New York, May 9, 1867.

cause wherein the interests of blacks and women inter-
sected, and that the historical timing was right for extend-
ing the franchise to both groups.

🐦 🐦 🐦

My friends, I am rejoiced that you are glad, but I
don't know how you will feel when I get through. I come
from another field—the country of the slave. They have
got their liberty—so much good luck to have slavery
partly destroyed; not entirely. I want it root and branch
destroyed. Then we will all be free indeed. I feel that if
I have to answer for the deeds done in my body just as
much as a man, I have a right to have just as much as a
man. There is a great stir about colored men getting
their rights, but not a word about the colored women;
and if colored men get their rights, and not colored
women theirs, you see the colored men will be masters
over the women, and it will be just as bad as it was before. So I am for keeping the thing going while things
are stirring; because if we wait till it is still, it will take a
great while to get it going again. White women are a
great deal smarter, and know more than colored women,
while colored women do not know scarcely anything.
They go out washing, which is about as high as a colored
woman gets, and their men go about idle, strutting up
and down; and take it all, and then scold because there
is no food. I want you consider on that, chil'n. I call you
chil'n; you are somebody's chil'n, and I am old enough
to be mother of all that is here. I want women to have
their rights. In the courts women have no right, no
voice; nobody speaks for them. I wish woman to have
her voice there among the pettifoggers. If it is not a fit
place for women, it is unfit for men to be there.

I am above eighty years old; it is about time for me to be going. I have been forty years a slave and forty years free and would be here forty years more to have equal rights for all. I suppose I am kept here because something remains for me to do; I suppose I am yet to help to break the chain. I have done a great deal of work; as much as a man, but did not get so much pay. I used to work in the field and bind grain, keeping up with the cradler; but men doing no more, got twice as much pay; so with the German women. They work in the field and do as much work, but do not get the pay. We do as much, we eat as much, we want as much. I suppose I am about the only colored woman that goes about to speak for the rights of colored women. I want to keep the thing stirring, now that the ice is cracked. What we want is a little money. You men know that you get as much again as women when you write, or for what you do. When we get our rights we shall not have to come to you for money, for then we shall have money enough in our own pockets; and may be you will ask us for money. But help us now until we get it. It is a good consolation to know that when we have got this battle once fought we shall not be coming to you any more. You have been having our rights so long, that you think, like a slaveholder, that you own us. I know that is hard for one who has held the reins for so long to give up; it cuts like a knife. It will feel all the better when it closes up again. I have been in Washington about three years, seeing about these colored people. Now colored men have the right to vote. There ought to be equal rights now more than ever, since colored people have got their freedom. I am going to talk several times while I am here; so now I will do a little singing. I have not heard any singing since I came here.

Appendix of Documents

Document 1: The Amazing Escape of Henry "Box" Brown

Henry "Box" Brown's famous mode of escape is recounted in the following selection from black abolitionist William Still's Underground Railroad Records, *published in 1872.*

Henry "Box" Brown escapes slavery by having himself nailed into a small box and shipped from Richmond to Philadelphia.

He was decidedly an unhappy piece of property in the city of Richmond, Va. In the condition of a slave he felt that it would be impossible for him to remain. Full well did he know, however, that it was no holiday task to escape the vigilance of Virginia slave-hunters, or the wrath of an enraged master for committing the unpardonable sin of attempting to escape to a land of liberty. So Brown counted well the cost before venturing upon his hazardous undertaking. Ordinary modes of travel he concluded might prove disastrous to his hopes; he, therefore, hit upon a new invention altogether, which was to have himself boxed up and forwarded to Philadelphia direct by express. The size of the box and how it was to be made to fit him most comfortably, was of his own ordering. Two feet eight inches deep, two feet wide, and three feet long were the exact dimensions of the box, lined with baize. His resources in regard to food and water consisted of the following: One bladder of water and a few small biscuits. His mechanical implement to meet the death-struggle for fresh air, all told, was one large gimlet. Satisfied that it would be far better to peril his life for freedom in this way than to remain under the galling yoke of Slavery, he entered his box, which was safely nailed up and hooped with five hickory hoops, and then was addressed by his next friend, James A. Smith, a shoe dealer, to Wm. H. Johnson, Arch Street, Philadelphia, marked, "This side up with care." In this condition he was sent to Adams' Express office in a dray, and thence by overland express to Philadelphia. It was twenty-six hours from the time he left Richmond until his arrival in the city of Brotherly Love. The notice, "This side up, etc.," did not avail with the different expressmen, who hesitated not to handle the box in the usual rough manner common to this class of men. For a while they actually had the box upside down, and had him on his head for miles. A few days before he was expected, certain intimation was conveyed to a member of the Vigilance Committee that a box might be expected by the three o'clock morning train from the South, which might contain a man.

All was quiet. The door had been safely locked. The proceedings commenced. Mr. [J.M.] McKim rapped quietly on the lid of the box and called out, "All right!" Instantly came the answer from within, "All right, sir!"

The witnesses will never forget that moment, Saw and hatchet quickly had the five hickory hoops cut and the lid off, and the marvelous resurrection of Brown ensued. Rising up in the box, he reached out his hand, saying, "How do you do, gentlemen?" the little assemblage hardly knew what to think or do at the moment. He was about as wet as if he had come up out of the Delaware. Very soon he remarked that, before leaving Richmond he had selected for his arrival hymn (if he lived) the Psalm beginning with these words: "I awaited patiently for the Lord, and He heard my prayer." And most touchingly did he sing the psalm, much to his own relief, as well as to the delight of his small audience.

William Still, *Underground Railroad Records.* Philadelphia, 1872. www.wm.edu/Whitman/slavery/analogue6.html.

Document 2: Against Racist Emigration Laws

James Forten (1767–1842), a self-made businessman and pamphleteer, was among the most influential early abolitionists. The following letter is excerpted from an 1813 pamphlet Forten wrote to protest Pennsylvania's proposed laws to restrict the free movement of blacks.

LETTERS From a MAN OF COLOUR, on a late Bill before the Senate of Pennsylvania.
LETTER I. O Liberty! thou power supremely bright,

Profuse of bliss and pregnant with delight,
Perpetual pleasures in thy presence reign,
And smiling Plenty leads thy wanton train Addison.

We hold this truth to be self-evident, that GOD created all men equal, and is one of the most prominent features in the Declaration of Independence, and in that glorious fabric of collected wisdom, our noble Constitution. This idea embraces the Indian and the European, the Savage and the Saint, the Peruvian and the Laplander, the white Man and the African, and whatever measures are adopted subversive of this inestimable privilege, are in direct violation of the letter and spirit of our Constitution, and become subject to the animadversion of all, particularly those who are deeply interested in the measure.

These thoughts were suggested by the promulgation of a late bill, before the Senate of Pennsylvania, to prevent the emigration of people of colour into this state. It was not passed into a law at this session and must in consequence lay over until the next, before when we sincerely hope, the white men, whom we should look upon as our protectors, will have become convinced of the inhumanity and impolicy of such a measure, and forbear to deprive us of those inestimable treasures, Liberty and Independence. This is almost the only state in the Union wherein the African have justly boasted of rational liberty and the protection of the laws, and shall it now be said they have been deprived of that liberty, and publicly exposed for sale to the highest bidder? Shall colonial inhumanity that has marked many of us with shameful stripes, become the practice of the people of Pennsylvania, while Mercy stands weeping at the miserable spectacle? People of Pennsylvania, descendants of the immortal [state founder William] Penn, doom us not to the unhappy fate of thousands of our countrymen in the Southern States and the West Indies; despise the traffic in blood, and the blessing of the African will forever be around you. Many of us are men of property, for the security of which, we have hitherto looked to the laws of our blessed state, but should this become a law, our property is jeopardized, since the same power which can expose to sale an unfortunate fellow creature, can wrest from him those estates which years of honest industry have accumulated. Where shall the poor African look for protection, should the people of Pennsylvania consent to oppress him? We grant there are a number of worthless men belonging to our colour, but there are laws of sufficient rigour for their punishment, if properly and duly enforced. We wish not to screen the guilty to not permit the innocent to suffer. If there are worthless men, there also men of merit among the African race, who are useful members of Society. The truth of this let their benevolent institutions and the numbers clothed and fed by them witness. Punish the guilty man of colour to the utmost limit of the laws, but sell him not to slavery! If he is in danger of becoming a public charge prevent him! If he is too indolent to labour for his own subsistence, compel him to do so; but sell him not slavery. By selling him you do not make him better, but commit a wrong, without benefiting the object of it or society at large. Many of our ancestors were brought here more than one hundred years ago; many of our fathers, many of ourselves, have fought and bled for the independence of our country. Do not then expose us to sale. Let not the spirit of the father behold the son robbed of that liberty which he died to establish, but let the motto of our legislators, be—"The Law knows no distinction."

These are only a few desultory remarks on the subject and intend to succeed this effervescence of feeling, by a series of essays, tending to prove the impolicy and unconstitutionality of the law in question.

For the present, I leave the public to the consideration of the above observations, in which I hope they will see so much truth, that they will never consent to sell to slavery.

James Forten, "Series of Letters by a Man of Colour," *Freedom's Journal*, February/March 1827, in *Pamphlets of Protest*, eds. Richard Newman, Patrick Rael, and Philip Lapsanksy. New York: Routledge, 2001, pp. 67–68.

Document 3: Proceedings of the New York Committee of Vigilance

The following excerpt is the preface to an 1837 document produced by members of the black abolitionist New York Committee of Vigilance. The document addresses the plight of fugitive slaves and reflects the high level of organization in the African American activist community.

The origin and object of the New York Committee of Vigilance are as follows: At a meeting of The Friends of Human Rights, held in the city of New York, Nov. 20, 1835, for the purpose of adopting measures to ascertain, if possible, the extent to which the cruel practice of kidnapping men, women and children, is carried on in this city, and to aid such unfortunate persons as may be in danger of being *reduced to Slavery*, in maintaining their rights—ROBERT BROWN, Esq. was called to the Chair, and David Ruggles, appointed Secretary.

The meeting being impressed with the alarming *fact* that any colored person within this State is liable to be arrested as a *fugitive from slavery* and put upon his defence to prove his freedom, and that any such person thus arrested is denied the *right of trial by jury*, and, therefore subject to a hurried trial, often without the aid of a friend or a counsellor—We hold ourselves bound by the Golden Rule of our Saviour, to aid them, to *do to others as we would have them do to us*. It is therefore,

Resolved, That William Johnston, David Ruggles, Robert Brown, George R. Barker, J.W. Higgins, be appointed a committee to aid the people of color, legally to obtain their rights.

Resolved, That this Committee be authorized to add to their number and to fill vacancies.

Resolved, That three members shall be a quorum at any meeting regularly called.

Resolved, That this meeting commend the Committee to the confidence of the people of color and to the liberality and support of the friends of Human Rights.

ROBERT BROWN, Chairman.

DAVID RUGGLES, Secretary

ANNUAL MEETING OF THE NEW YORK COM-
MITTEE OF VIGILANCE.—A public meeting will be
held, in aid of the people of Color, tomorrow evening, January 16th, at the Third Presbyterian Church, corner of
Thompson and Houston streets, to commence at seven o'-
clock precisely. The attendance of the public is respectfully
invited.

W. JOHNSTON, Chairman of Committee of Arrange-
ments.

We, the Committee appointed by the said meeting, being
deeply impressed with the important and urgent nature of
the duties committed to us, earnestly solicit the aid of the
friends of humanity for the accomplishment of the following
objects

1. To protect unoffending, defenceless, and endangered
persons of color, by securing their rights as far as practicable.

2. By obtaining for them when arrested, under the pretext
of being *fugitive slaves*, such protection as the law will afford.

These objects are so continually pressing themselves on
the notice of the friends of our colored brethren especially
in the City of New York, that we feel compelled by the dic-
tates of humanity, and by the authority of God to exert ourselves in their behalf, and therefore we appeal to you, to *aid*
in this work of philanthropy and Christian benevolence.

"New York Committee of Vigilance for the Year 1837, Together with Important
Facts Relative to Their Proceedings," in *Pamphlets of Protest*, eds. Richard Newman,
Patrick Rael, and Philip Lapsansky. New York: Routledge, 2001, pp. 145–46.

Document 4: The Black Citizens of Pennsylvania Organize

*Robert Purvis (1810–1898) was, like James Forten, a wealthy
abolitionist active in Philadelphia's black community and the Underground Railroad. In the following excerpt Purvis protests the
denial of voting rights to blacks dictated by the 1837 Pennsylvania
Constitutional Convention.*

It is notorious that many whites who were forsaken by their
own relations and left to the mercy of . . . disease, were

nursed gratuitously by the colored people. Does this speak an enmity which would abuse the privileges of civil liberty to the injury of the whites? We have the testimony of a committee of the Senate of this commonwealth, no longer ago than 1830, who were appointed to report upon the expediency of restricting the emigration of colored people into the commonwealth. The following extract from their report, signed by Hon. Mr. Breck, chairman, testifies to our character: "On this subject your committee beg to remark, that by the last census our colored population amounted to about 36,000 of whom 30,000 inhabit the eastern district and only 6,000 the western. And this number, so small compared with the white population, is scattered among 1,500,000 of our own color, making 1 colored to 42 whites. So few of these, it is believed by your committee, need not at present be an object of uneasiness, and would not seem to require the enactment of any restrictive laws, MORE ESPECIALLY AS THEY ARE FOR THE GREATER PART, INDUSTRIOUS, PEACEABLE, AND USEFUL PEOPLE."

Be it remembered, fellow citizens, that it is only the "industrious, peaceable, and useful" part of the colored people that we plead. We would have the right of suffrage only as the reward of industry and worth. We care not how high the qualification be placed. All we ask, is that no man shall be excluded on account of his color, that the same rule shall be applied to all.

Are we to be disfranchised, lest the purity of the *white* blood should be sullied by an intermixture with ours? It seems to us that our white brethren might well enough reserve their fear, till we seek such alliance with them. We ask no social favors. We would not willingly darken the doors of those to whom the complexion and features, which our Maker has given us, are disagreeable. The territories of the commonwealth are sufficiently ample to afford us a home without doing violence to the delicate nerves of our white brethren, for centuries to come. Besides, we are not intruders here, nor, were our ancestors. Surely you ought to bear as unrepiningly the evil consequences of your fathers' guilt, of our father's misfortune. Proscription and disfranchisement are the last things in the world to alleviate these evil consequences. Nothing, as shameful experience has already proved, can so powerfully promote the evil which you profess to deprecate, as the degradation of our race by the oppressive rule of yours. Give us that fair and honorable ground which self-respect requires us to stand on, and the dreaded amalgamation, if it takes place at all, shall be by your own fault, as indeed it has always been. We dare not give full vent to the indignation we feel on this point, but we will not attempt wholly to conceal it. . . .

Fellow citizens, willl you take the first step towards reimposing the chains which have now rusted for more than fifty years? Need we inform you that every colored man in Pennsylvania is exposed to be arrested as a fugitive from slavery? and that it depends not upon the verdict of a jury of his peers, but upon the decision of a judge on summary process, whether or not he shall be dragged into southern bondage? The Constitution of the United States provides that "no person shall be deprived of life, liberty, or property, without due process of law"—by which is certainly meant a TRIAL BY JURY. Yet the act of Congress of 1793, for the recovery of fugitive slaves, authorizes the claimant to seize his victim without a warrant from any magistrate, and allows him to drag him before "any magistrate of a county, city, or town corporate, where such seizure has been made," and upon proving, by "oral testimony or affidavit," to the satisfaction of such magistrate that the man is his slave, gives him a right to take him into everlasting bondage.

Thus may a free-born citizen of Pennsylvania be arrested, tried without counsel, jury, or power to call witnesses, condemned by a single man, and carried across Mason and Dixon's line, within the compass of a single day. An act of this commonwealth, passed 1820, and enlarged and re-enacted in 1825, it is true, puts some restraint upon the power of the claimant under the act of Congress; but it still leaves the case to the decision of a single judge, without the privilege of a jury! What unspeakably aggravates our loss of the right of suffrage at this moment is, that, while the increased activity of the slave-catchers enhances our danger, the Reform Convention has refused to amend the Constitution so as to protect our liberty by a jury trial! We entreat you to make our case your own—imagine your own wives and children to be trembling at the approach of every stranger, lest their husbands and fathers should be dragged into a slavery worse than Algerine—worse than death! Fellow citizens, if there is one of us who has abused the right of suffrage, let him be tried and punished according to law. But in the name of humanity, in the name of justice, in the name of the God you profess to worship, who has no respect of persons, do not turn into gall and wormwood the friendship we bear to yourselves by ratifying a Constitution which tears from us a privilege dearly earned and, inestimably prized. We lay hold of the principles which Pennsylvania asserted in the hour which tried men's souls—which BENJAMIN FRANKLIN and his eight colleagues, in name of the commonwealth, pledged their lives, their fortunes, and their sacred honor to sustain: We take our stand upon that solemn declaration; that to protect inalienable rights "governments are instituted among men, deriving their JUST POWERS from the CONSENT of the governed," and proclaim that a government which tears away from us and our posterity the very power of CONSENT, is a tyrannical usurpation which we will never cease to oppose. We have seen with amazement and grief the apathy of white Pennsylvanians while the "Reform Convention" has been perpetrating this outrage upon the good old principles of Pennsylvania freedom. But however others may forsake these principles, we promise to maintain them on *Pennsylvania soil*, to the last man. If this disfranchisement is designed to uproot us, it shall jail Pennsylvania's fields, valleys, mountains, and rivers; her canals, railroads, forests, and mines; her domestic altars, and her public, religious and benevolent institutions; . . . her consecrated past and her brilliant future, are as dear to us as they can be to you. Firm upon our Pennsylvania BILL OF RIGHTS, and trusting in a God of Truth and justice, we lay our claim before you, with the warning that no amendments of the present Constitution can compensate for the loss of its foundation principle of equal rights, nor for the conversion into enemies of 40,000 friends.

Robert Purvis, *The Colored American*, in *Pamphlets of Protest*, eds. in Richard Newman, Patrick Rael, and Philip Lapsanksy. New York: Routledge, 2001, pp. 133–134.

Document 5: Life in Canada for Black Emigrants

Mary Ann Shadd (1823–1893) was a teacher, writer, and abolitionist who immigrated to Canada in the early 1850s. In the following excerpt Shadd sums up the benefits of Canadian emigration for other blacks seeking freedom, especially in the aftermath of the stringent Fugitive Slave Law of 1850.

The increasing desire on the part of the colored people, to become thoroughly informed respecting the Canadas, and particularly that part of the province called Canada West—to learn of the climate, soil, and productions, and of the inducements offered generally to emigrants, and to them particularly, since that the passage of the odious Fugitive Slave Law has made a residence in the United States to many of them dangerous to the extreme,—this consideration, and the absence of condensed information accessible to all, is my excuse for offering this tract to the notice of the public. The people are in a strait,—on the one hand, a pro-slavery administration, with its entire controllable force, is bearing upon them with fatal effect: on the other, the Colonization Society, in the garb of *Christianity* and *Philanthropy*, is seconding the efforts of the first named power, by bringing into the lists a vast social and immoral influence, thus making more effective the agencies employed. Information is needed.—Tropical Africa, the land of promise of the colonizationists, teeming as she is with the breath of pestilence, a burning sun and fearful maladies, bids them welcome;—she feelingly invites to moral and physical death, under a voluntary escort of their most bitter enemies at home. Again, many look with dreadful forebodings to the probability of worse than inquisitorial inhumanity in the Southern States from the operation of the Fugitive Law. Certain that neither a home in Africa, nor in the Southern States, is desirable under present circumstances, inquiry is made respecting Canada. I have endeavored to furnish information to a certain extent, to that end, and believing that more reliance would be placed upon a statement of facts obtained in the country, from reliable sources and from observation, than upon a repetition of current statements made elsewhere, however honestly made, I determined to visit Canada, and to there collect such information as most persons desire. These pages contain the result of much inquiry—matter obtained both from individuals and from documents and papers of unquestionable character in the Province. . . .

The conclusion arrived at in respect to Canada, by an impartial person, is, that no settled country in America offers stronger inducements to colored people. The climate is healthy, and they enjoy as good health as other settlers, or as the natives; the soil is of the first quality; the laws of the country give to them, at first, the same protection and privileges as to other persons not born subjects; and after compliance with Acts of Parliament affecting them, as taking oath, &c., they many enjoy full "privileges of British birth in the Province." The general tone of society is healthy; vice is discountenanced, and infractions of the law promptly punished; and, added to this, there is an increasing anti-slavery sentiment, and a progressive system of religion. . . .

The question whether or not an extensive emigration by the free colored people of the United States would affect the institution of slavery, would then be answered. I have here taken the affirmative of that question, because that view of the case seems to me most clear. The free colored people have steadily discountenanced any rational scheme of emigration, in the hope that by remaining in the States, a powerful miracle for the overthrow of slavery would be wrought. What are the facts. More territory has been given up to slavery, the Fugitive Law has passed, and a concert of measures, seriously affecting their personal liberty, has been entered into by several of the Free states; so subtle, unseen and effective have been their movements, that, were it not that we remember there is a Great Britain, we would be overwhelmed, powerless, from the force of such successive shocks; and the end may not be yet, if we persist in remaining for targets, while they are strengthening themselves in the Northwest, and in the Gulf. There would be more of the right spirit, and infinitely more of real manliness, in a peaceful but decided demand for freedom to the slave from the Gulf of Mexico, than in a miserable scampering from state to state, in a vain endeavor to gather the crumbs of freedom that a pro-slavery besom may sweep away at any moment. May a selection for the best be made, now that there are countries between which and the United States a comparison may be instituted. A little folding of the hands, and there may be a retreat from the clutches of the slave power.

Mary Ann Shadd, *A Plea for Emigration, or Notes of Canada West, in Its Moral, Social, and Political Aspect: With Suggestions Respecting Mexico, West Indies, and Vancouver Island, for the Information of Colored Emigrants.* Detroit: George W. Pattison, 1852.

Document 6: A Failed Escape Is Punished

William Wells Brown (1814–1880) was a major literary figure who wrote fiction, drama, travel narrative, and essays. His novel Clotel *was the first novel published by an African American. He was also an influential abolitionist and former slave who describes, in the following excerpt from his autobiography, the punishment he received for an unsuccessful escape attempt.*

My mother was hired out in the city, and I was also hired out there to Major Freeland, who kept a public house. He was formerly from Virginia, and was a horse-racer, cock-fighter, gambler, and withal an inveterate drunkard. There were ten or twelve servants in the house, and when he was present, it was cut and slash—knock down and drag out. In his fits of anger, he would take up a chair, and throw it at a servant; and in his more rational moments, when he wished to chastise one, he would tie them up in the smokehouse, and whip them; after which, he would cause a fire to be made of tobacco stems, and smoke them. This he called "Virginia play."

I complained to my master of the treatment which I received from Major Freeland; but it made no difference. He cared nothing about it, so long as he received the money for my labor. After living with Major Freeland five or six months, I ran away, and went into the woods back of the city; and when night came on, I made my way to my master's farm, knowing that if Mr. Haskell, the overseer, should discover me, I should be again carried back to Major Freeland; so I kept in the woods. One day, while in the woods, I heard the barking and howling of dogs, and in a short time they came so near that I knew them to be the bloodhounds of Major Benjamin O'Fallon. He kept five or six, to hunt runaway slaves with. As soon as I was convinced that it was them, I knew there was no chance of escape. I took refuge in the top of a tree and the hounds were soon at its base, and there remained until the hunters came up in a half or three quarters of an hour afterwards. There were two men with the dogs, who, as soon as they came up, ordered me to descend. I came down, was tied, and taken to St. Louis jail. Major Freeland soon made his appearance, and took me out, and ordered me to follow him, which I did. After we returned home I was tied up in the smokehouse, and was very severely whipped. After the major had flogged me to his satisfaction, he sent out his son Robert, a young man eighteen or twenty years of age, to see that I was well smoked. He made a fire of tobacco stems, which soon set me to coughing and sneezing. This, Robert told me, was the way his father used to do to his slaves in Virginia. After giving me what they conceived to be a decent smoking, I was untied and again set to work.

William Wells Brown, *Narrative of William W. Brown, a Fugitive Slave Written by Himself*. Boston: Anti-Slavery Office, 1847.

Document 7: Two Poems About Slavery

Frances Ellis Watkins Harper (1825–1911) was among the most accomplished women of nineteenth-century America. She was a poet, novelist, and educator as well as a dedicated abolitionist and women's rights activist. The following two poems by Harper, "The Slave Mother" and "Bible Defence of Slavery," demonstrate the power of traditional literary forms, along with pamphlets and political essays, in conveying the grievous human toll exacted by the slave system.

"The Slave Mother"

Heard you that shriek? It rose
So wildly on the air,
It seem'd as if a burden'd heart
Was breaking in despair.
Saw you those hands so sadly clasped—
The bowed and feeble head—
The shuddering of that fragile form—
That look of grief and dread?

Saw you the sad, imploring eye?
Its every glance was pain,
As if a storm of agony
Were sweeping through the brain.
She is a mother pale with fear,
Her boy clings to her side,
And in her kyrtle vainly tries
His trembling form to hide.
He is not hers, although she bore
For him a mother's pains;
He is not hers, although her blood
is coursing through his veins!
He is not hers, for cruel hands
May rudely tear apart
The only wreath of household love
That binds her breaking heart.
His love has been a joyous light
That o'er her pathway smiled,
A fountain gushing ever new,
Amid life's desert wild.
His lightest word has been a tone
Of music round her heart,
Their lives a streamlet blent in one—
Oh, Father! must they part?

They tear him from her circling arms,
Her last and fond embrace:—
Oh! never more may her sad eyes
Gaze on his mournful face.
No marvel, then, these bitter shrieks

Disturb the listening air;
She is a mother, and her heart
Is breaking in despair.

"Bible Defence of Slavery"

Take sackcloth of the darkest dye,
And shroud the pulpits round!
Servants of Him that cannot lie,
Sit mourning on the ground.
Let holy horror blanch each cheek,
Pale every brow with fears;
And rocks and stones, if ye could speak,
Ye well might melt to tears!
Let sorrow breathe in every tone,
In every strain ye raise;
Insult not God's majestic throne
With th' mockery of praise

A "reverend" man, whose light should be
The guide of age and youth,
Brings to the shrine of Slavery
The sacrifice of truth!
For the direst wrong by man imposed,
Since Sodom's fearful cry,
The word of life has been unclos'd,
To give your God the lie.
Oh! when ye pray for heathen lands,
And plead for their dark shores,
Remember Slavery's cruel hands
Make heathens at your doors!

Frances E. W. Harper, "The Slave Mother" and "Bible Defence of Slavery," Black Heritage Library Collection. http://authorsdirectory.com/copyright.htm.

Document 8: Anthony Burns Speaks About His Capture

Runaway slave Anthony Burns (1834?–1862) escaped from Virginia to Boston in March of 1854. His capture two months later provoked violent riots and inspired twenty thousand Bostonians to march in protest through the streets. Burns's apprehension by authorities proved to be a watershed moment that galvanized abolitionist opposition to the Fugitive Slave Law; so massive was the uproar that Burns was the last fugitive that Massachusetts would ever send back into slavery. After abolitionists raised money to buy Burns's freedom in 1855, Burns delivered the following statement.

My friends, I am very glad to have it to say, have it to feel, that I am once more in the land of liberty; that I am with those who are my friends. Until my tenth year I did not care what became of me; but soon after I began to learn that there is a Christ who came to make us free; I began to hear about a North, and to feel the necessity for freedom of soul and body. I heard of a North where men of my color could live without any man daring to say to them, "You are my property;" and I determined by the blessing of God, one day to find my way there. My inclination grew on me, and I found my way to Boston.

You see, I didn't want to make myself known, so I didn't tell who I was; but as I came to work, I got employment, and I worked hard; but I kept my own counsel, and didn't tell anybody that I was a slave, but I strove for myself as I never had an opportunity to do before. When I was going home one night I heard some one running behind me; presently a hand was put on my shoulder, and somebody said: "Stop, stop; you are the fellow who broke into a silversmith's shop the other night." I assured the man that it was a mistake, but almost before I could speak, I was lifted from off my feet by six or seven others, and it was no use to resist. In the Court House I waited some time, and as the silversmith did not come, I told them I wanted to go home for supper. A man then come to the door; he didn't open it like an honest man would, but kind of slowly opened it, and looked in. He said, "How do you do, Mr. Burns?" and I called him as we do in Virginia, "master!"

He asked me if there would be any trouble in taking me back to Virginia, and I was brought right to a stand, and didn't know what to say. He wanted to know if I remembered the money that he used to give me, and I said, "Yes, I do recollect that you used to give me twelve and a half cents at the end of every year I worked for you." He went out and came back next morning. I got no supper nor sleep that night. The next morning they told me that my master said that he had the right to me, and as I had called him "master," having the fear of God before my eyes, I could not go from it. Next morning I was taken down, with the bracelets on my wrists—not such as you wear, ladies, of gold and silver—but iron and steel, that wore into the bone.

N.Y. Tribune, n.d., in the *Liberator*, March 9, 1855.

Document 9: Everyday Life Under Slavery

Abolitionist orator, writer, and Methodist minister Josiah Henson (1789–1883) spent his first forty-one years as a slave before escaping to freedom in Canada with his family. His 1849 autobiography, excerpted in the following passage, is widely believed to have inspired Harriet Beecher Stowe's Uncle Tom.

My earliest employments were, to carry buckets of water to the men at work, and to hold a horse-plough, used for weeding between the rows of corn. As I grew older and taller, I was entrusted with the care of master's saddle-horse. Then a hoe was put into my hands, and I was soon required to do the day's work of a man; and it was not long before I could do it, at least as well as my associates in misery.

A description of the everyday life of a slave on a southern plantation illustrates the character and habits of the slave and the slaveholder, created and perpetuated by their relative position. The principal food of those upon my master's plantation consisted of corn-meal and salt herrings; to which was added in summer a little buttermilk, and the few vegetables which each might raise for himself and his family, on the little piece of ground which was assigned to him for the purpose, called a truck-patch.

In ordinary times we had two regular meals in a day: breakfast at twelve o'clock, after laboring from daylight, and supper when the work of the remainder of the day was over. In harvest season we had three. Our dress was of tow-cloth; for the children, nothing but a shirt; for the older ones a pair of pantaloons or a gown in addition, according to the sex. Besides these, in the winter a round jacket or overcoat, a wool-hat once in two or three years, for the males, and a pair of coarse shoes once a year. We lodged in log huts, and on the bare ground. Wooden floors were an unknown luxury. In a single room were huddled, like cattle, ten or a dozen persons, men, women, and children. All ideas of refinement and decency were, of course, out of the question. We had neither bedsteads, nor furniture of any description. Our beds were collections of straw and old rags, thrown down in the corners and boxed in with boards; a single blanket the only covering. Our favourite way of sleeping, however, was on a plank, our heads raised on an old jacket and our feet toasting before the smouldering fire. The wind whistled and the rain and snow blew in through the cracks, and the damp earth soaked in the moisture till the floor was miry as a pig-sty. Such were our houses. In these wretched hovels were we penned at night, and fed by day; here were the children born and the sick—neglected.

Josiah Henson, *"Uncle Tom's Story of His Life": An Autobiography of the Rev. Josiah Henson*. London, 1877. http://aalbc.com/authors/josiah.htm.

Document 10: A Call to Resistance

Minister and orator Henry Highland Garnet (1815–1881) was among the more radical black abolitionists in that he believed that violent resistance was a legitimate, even necessary tactic in the fight against slavery. The following excerpt is from his famous 1843 speech delivered at an antislavery convention in Buffalo, New York. Garnet's exhortation of slaves to rise up against their oppressors divided the abolitionist movement and drove a philosophical wedge between Garnet and fellow black leader Frederick Douglass.

Brethren, arise, arise! Strike for your lives and liberties. Now is the day and the hour. Let every slave throughout the land do this and the days of slavery are numbered. You cannot be more oppressed than you have been—you cannot suffer greater cruelties than you have already. *Rather die freemen than live to be slaves.* Remember that you are FOUR MILLIONS! It is in your power so to torment the God-cursed slave-holders that they will be glad to let you go free. If the scale was turned, and black men were the masters and white men the slaves, every destructive agent and element would be employed to lay the oppressor low. Danger and death would hang over their heads day and night. Yes, the tyrants would meet with plagues more terrible than those of Pharaoh. But you are a patient people. You act as though, you were made for the special use of these devils. You act as though your daughters were born to pamper the lusts of your masters and overseers. And worse than all, you tamely submit while your lords tear your wives from your embraces and defile them before your eyes. In the name of God, we ask you, are you men? Where is the blood of your fathers? Has it all run out of your veins? Awake, awake; millions of voices are calling you! Your dead fathers speak to you from their graves. Heaven, as with a voice of thunder, calls on you to arise from the dust.

Let your motto be resistance! *resistance!* RESISTANCE! No oppressed people have ever secured their liberty without resistance. What kind of resistance you had better make, you must decide by the circumstances that surround you, and according to the suggestion of expediency. Brethren, adieu! Trust in the living God. Labor for the peace of the human race, and remember that you are FOUR MILLIONS.

Henry Highland Garnet, "An Address to the Slaves of the United States of America," in *Negro Orators and Their Orations*, ed. Carter G. Woodson. Washington, DC. Associated, 1925.

Document 11: The Fugitive Slave Law

The Fugitive Slave Law of 1850, excerpted in the following passage, was enacted as part of the compromise act that allowed California's admission to the Union as a free state. One of several concessions provided to proslavery interests by the act, the new Fugitive Slave Law exceeded previous statutes by criminalizing the assistance of runaways along with the act of escape.

Chap. LX.—An Act to amend, and supplementary to the Act

entitled "An Act respecting Fugitives from Justice, and Persons escaping from the Service of their Masters," approved February twelfth, one thousand seven hundred and ninety-three. . . . When a person held to service or labor in any State or Territory of the United States, has heretofore or shall hereafter escape into another State or Territory of the United States, the person or persons to whom such service or labor may be due, or his, her, or their agent or attorney, duly authorized, by power of attorney, in writing, acknowledged and certified under the seal of some legal officer or court of the State or Territory in which the same may be executed, may pursue and reclaim such fugitive person, either by procuring a warrant from some one of the courts, judges, or commissioners aforesaid, of the proper circuit, district, or county, for the apprehension of such fugitive from service or labor, or by seizing and arresting such fugitive, where the same can be done without process, and by taking, or causing such person to be taken, forthwith before such court, judge, or commissioner, whose duty it shall be to hear and determine the case of such claimant in a summary manner; and upon satisfactory proof being made, by deposition or affidavit, in writing, to be taken and certified by such court, judge, or commissioner, or by other satisfactory testimony, duly taken and certified by some court, magistrate, justice of the peace, or other legal officer authorized to administer an oath and take depositions under the laws of the State or Territory from which such person owing service or labor may have escaped, with a certificate of such magistracy or other authority, as aforesaid, with the seal of the proper court or officer thereto attached, which seal shall be sufficient to establish the competency of the proof, and with proof, also by affidavit, of the identity of the person whose service or labor is claimed to be due as aforesaid, that the person so arrested does in fact owe service or labor to the person or persons claiming him or her, in the State or Territory from which such fugitive may have escaped as aforesaid, and that said person escaped, to make out and deliver to such claimant, his or her agent or attorney, a certificate setting forth the substantial facts as to the service or labor due from such fugitive to the claimant, and of his or her escape from the State or Territory in which he or she was arrested, with authority to such claimant, or his or her agent or attorney, to use such reasonable force and restraint as may be necessary, under the circumstances of the case, to take and remove such fugitive person back to the State or Territory whence he or she may have escaped as aforesaid. In no trial or hearing under this act shall the testimony of such alleged fugitive be admitted in evidence; and the certificates in this and the first [fourth] section mentioned, shall be conclusive of the right of the person or persons in whose favor granted, to remove such fugitive to the State or Territory from which he escaped, and shall prevent all molestation of such person or persons by any process issued by any court, judge, magistrate, or other person whomsoever.

SEC. 7. And be it further enacted, That any person who shall knowingly and willingly obstruct, hinder, or prevent such claimant, his agent or attorney, or any person or persons lawfully assisting him, her, or them, from arresting such a fugitive from service or labor, either with or without process as aforesaid, or shall rescue, or attempt to rescue, such fugitive from service or labor, from the custody of such claimant, his or her agent or attorney, or other person or persons lawfully assisting as aforesaid, when so arrested, pursuant to the authority herein given and declared; or shall aid, abet, or assist such person so owing service or labor as aforesaid, directly or indirectly, to escape from such claimant, his agent or attorney, or other person or persons legally authorized as aforesaid; or shall harbor or conceal such fugitive, so as to prevent the discovery and arrest of such person, after notice or knowledge of the fact that such person was a fugitive from service or labor as aforesaid, shall, for either of said offences, be subject to a fine not exceeding one thousand dollars, and imprisonment not exceeding six months, by indictment and conviction before the District Court of the United States for the district in which such offence may have been committed, or before the proper court of criminal jurisdiction, if committed within any one of the organized Territories of the United States; and shall moreover forfeit and pay, by way of civil damages to the party injured by such illegal conduct, the sum of one thousand dollars for each fugitive so lost as aforesaid, to be recovered by action of debt, in any of the District or Territorial Courts aforesaid, within whose jurisdiction the said offence may have been committed.

Fugitive Slave Act of 1850, 31st Cong., 1st sess., September 18, 1850.

Document 12: Dred Scott Must Remain a Slave

The Dred Scott decision of 1857, excerpted in the following selection, struck a crushing blow to the abolitionist movement. In the decision Supreme Court justice Roger B. Taney ruled that blacks "had no rights the white man was bound to respect," overturning the free-state/slave-state balance established by the Missouri Compromise of 1820 and effectively denying blacks the legal status of citizenship.

The question is simply this: can a negro whose ancestors were imported into this country and sold as slaves, become a member of the political community formed and brought into existence by the Constitution of the United States, and as such become entitled to all the rights, and privileges, and immunities, guarantied by that instrument to the citizen. One of these rights is the privilege of suing in a court of the United States in the cases specified in the Constitution. . . .

The words "people of the United States" and "citizens" are synonymous terms, and mean the same thing. They both describe the political body who, according to our republican institutions, form the sovereignty, and who hold the power and conduct the government through their representatives. They are what we familiarly call the "sovereign people," and every citizen is one of this people, and a constituent member of this sovereignty. The question before us is, whether the class of persons described in the plea of abatement compose a portion of this people, and are constituent members of this sovereignty. We think they are not, and that they are not included, and were not intended to be included, under the word "citizens" in the Constitution, and can, therefore, claim none of the rights and privileges which that instrument provides for and secures to citizens of the United

States. On the contrary, they were at that time considered as a subordinate and inferior class of beings, who had been subjugated by the dominant race, and whether emancipated or not, yet remained subject to their authority, and had no rights or privileges but such as those who held the power and the government might choose to grant them. . . .

A perpetual and impassable barrier was intended to be erected between the white race and the one which they had reduced to slavery, and governed as subjects with absolute and despotic power, and which they then looked upon as so far below them in the scale of created beings, that intermarriages between white persons and negroes or mulattoes were regarded as unnatural and immoral, and punished as crimes, not only in the parties, but in the person who joined them in marriage. And no distinction in this respect was made between the free negro or mulatto and the slave, but this stigma, of the deepest degradation, was fixed upon the whole race. . . .

No one, we presume, supposed that any change in public opinion or feeling, in relation to this unfortunate race, in the civilized nations of Europe or in this country, should induce the court to give to the words of the Constitution a more liberal construction in their favor than they were intended to bear when the instrument was framed and adopted. Such an argument would be altogether inadmissible in any tribunal called out to interpret it. If any of its provisions are deemed unjust, there is a mode prescribed in the instrument itself by which it may be amended; but while it remains unaltered, it must be construed now as it was understood at the time of its adoption. It is not only the same in words, but the same in meaning, and delegates the same powers to the government, and reserves and secures the same rights and privileges to the citizen; and as long as it continues to exist in its present form, it speaks not only in the same words, but with the same meaning and intent with which it spoke when it came from the hands of its framers, and was voted on and adopted by the people of the United States. Any other rule of construction would abrogate the judicial character of this court, and make it the mere reflex of the popular opinion or passion of the day. This court was not created by the Constitution for such purposes. Higher and graver trusts have been confided to it, and it must not falter in the path of duty. . . .

The powers over person and property of which we speak are not only not granted to Congress, but are in express terms denied, and they are forbidden to exercise them. And this prohibition is not confined to the States, but the words are general, and extend to the whole territory over which the Constitution gives it power to legislate, including those portions of it remaining under territorial government, as well as that covered by States. It is a total absence of power everywhere within the dominion of the United States, and places the citizens of a territory, so far as these rights are concerned, on the same footing with citizens of the States, and guards them as firmly and plainly against any inroads which the general government might attempt, under the plea of implied or incidental powers. And if Congress itself cannot do this—if it is beyond the powers conferred on the Federal Government—it will be admitted, we presume, that it could not authorize a territorial government to exercise them. It could confer no power on any local government, established by its authority, to violate the provisions of the Constitution.

It seems, however, to be supposed, that there is a difference between property in a slave and other property, and that different rules may be applied to it in expounding the Constitution of the United States. And the laws and usages of nations, and the writings of eminent jurists upon the relation of master and slave and their mutual rights and duties, and the powers which governments may exercise over it, have been dwelt upon in the argument.

But in considering the question before us, it must be borne in mind that there is no law of nations standing between the people of the United States and their government and interfering with their relation to each other. The powers of the government and the rights of the citizen under it, are positive and practical regulations plainly written down. The people of the United States have delegated to it certain enumerated powers, and forbidden it to exercise others. It has no power over the person or property of a citizen but what the citizens of the United States have granted. And no laws or usages of other nations, or reasoning of statesmen or jurists upon the relations of master and slave, can enlarge the powers of the government, or take from the citizens the rights they have reserved. And if the Constitution recognizes the right of property of the master in a slave, and makes no distinction between that description of property and other property owned by a citizen, no tribunal, acting under the authority of the United States, whether it be legislative, executive, or judicial, has a right to draw such a distinction, or deny to it the benefit of the provisions and guarantees which have been provided for the protection of private property against the encroachments of the government.

Roger B. Taney, U.S. Supreme Court decision in *Dred Scott v. Sandford*, March 1857.

Document 13: The Emancipation Proclamation

Abraham Lincoln issued a preliminary Emancipation Proclamation on September 22, 1862, declaring that unless the seceded states abandoned their rebellion, all slaves in the Confederacy would be permanently freed on the following January 1. Although Lincoln's decree pointedly exempted slaves in loyal border states, the Emancipation Proclamation was still widely heralded by northern abolitionists and denounced by outraged Confederates.

Whereas on the 22nd day of September, A.D. 1862, a proclamation was issued by the President of the United States, containing, among other things, the following, to wit:

"That on the 1st day of January, A.D. 1863, all persons held as slaves within any State or designated part of a State the people whereof shall then be in rebellion against the United States shall be then, thenceforward, and forever free; and the executive government of the United States, including the military and naval authority thereof, will recognize and maintain the freedom of such persons and will do no act or acts to repress such persons, or any of them, in any efforts they may make for their actual freedom.

"That the executive will on the 1st day of January aforesaid, by proclamation, designate the States and parts of States, if any, in which the people thereof, respectively, shall then be in rebellion against the United States; and the fact that any State or the people thereof shall on that day be in good faith represented in the Congress of the United States by members chosen thereto at elections wherein a majority of the qualified voters of such States shall have participated shall, in the absence of strong countervailing testimony, be deemed conclusive evidence that such State and the people thereof are not then in rebellion against the United States."

Now, therefore, I, Abraham Lincoln, President of the United States, by virtue of the power in me vested as Commander-In-Chief of the Army and Navy of the United States in time of actual armed rebellion against the authority and government of the United States, and as a fit and necessary war measure for supressing said rebellion, do, on this 1st day of January, A.D. 1863, and in accordance with my purpose so to do, publicly proclaimed for the full period of one hundred days from the first day above mentioned, order and designate as the States and parts of States wherein the people thereof, respectively, are this day in rebellion against the United States the following, to wit:

Arkansas, Texas, Louisiana (except the parishes of St. Bernard, Palquemines, Jefferson, St. John, St. Charles, St. James, Ascension, Assumption, Terrebone, Lafourche, St. Mary, St. Martin, and Orleans, including the city of New Orleans), Mississippi, Alabama, Florida, Georgia, South Carolina, North Carolina, and Virginia (except the forty-eight counties designated as West Virginia, and also the counties of Berkeley, Accomac, Morthhampton, Elizabeth City, York, Princess Anne, and Norfolk, including the cities of Norfolk and Portsmouth), and which excepted parts are for the present left precisely as if this proclamation were not issued.

And by virtue of the power and for the purpose aforesaid, I do order and declare that all persons held as slaves within said designated States and parts of States are, and henceforward shall be, free; and that the Executive Government of the United States, including the military and naval authorities thereof, will recognize and maintain the freedom of said persons.

And I hereby enjoin upon the people so declared to be

free to abstain from all violence, unless in necessary self-defence; and I recommend to them that, in all case when allowed, they labor faithfully for reasonable wages.

And I further declare and make known that such persons of suitable condition will be received into the armed service of the United States to garrison forts, positions, stations, and other places, and to man vessels of all sorts in said service.

And upon this act, sincerely believed to be an act of justice, warranted by the Constitution upon military necessity, I invoke the considerate judgment of mankind and the gracious favor of Almighty God.

Abraham Lincoln, *The Collected Works of Abraham Lincoln*, vol. 6. ed. Roy P. Basler. New Brunswick, NJ: Rutgers University Press, 1953, pp. 28–30.

Document 14: Blacks Deserve the Right to Vote

Lawyer, educator, and activist John Mercer Langston (1829–1897) became the first black American to hold elected office as town clerk in Ohio. Later in his distinguished public career he served as an American diplomat in Haiti and, briefly, as U.S congressman from Virginia. Twice his name was seriously considered for vice president on the Republican ticket. Like many prominent black abolitionists, Langston regarded voting rights as imperative to the cause of black equality, as is demonstrated in the following excerpt from a speech he delivered in Missouri less than a year after the end of the Civil War.

To every true, honest, and liberty-loving citizen of Missouri do the colored men of your redeemed Commonwealth appeal for sympathy and aid in securing those political rights and privileges which belong to us as free men. . . .

Our demands are not excessive.

We ask not for social equality with the white man, as is often claimed by the shallow demagogue; for a law higher than human must forever govern social relations.

We ask only that privilege which is now given to the very poorest and meanest of white men who come to the ballot-box.

We demand this as those who are native-born citizens of

this State, and have never known other allegiance than to its authority and to these United States.

We demand this in the names of those whose bitter toil has enriched our State and brought wealth to its homes.

We demand this as those who have ever cheerfully sustained law and order, and who have, within our means, zealously promoted education and morality.

We demand this as those who have been true and loyal to our Government from its foundation to the present, and who have never deserted its interests while even in the midst of treason and under subjection to its most violent enemies.

We demand this in the honored name of the nine thousand colored troops who, with the first opportunity, enlisted under the banner of Missouri and bared their breasts to the remorseless storm of treason, and by hundreds went down to death in the conflict, while the franchised rebel, the cowardly conservative—the now bitterest enemies of our right to suffrage—remained in quiet at home, safe, and fattened on the fruits of our sacrifice, toil, and blood.

In the names of the heroic dead who, from Missouri's colored troops, were left on the battle-field of Oxford—in the campaign against Mobile—in the battle at Blakely—at the fierce engagement on the Rio Grande—and who along every line of skirmish were like brutes shot down by savage rebels—do We appeal for the simple privilege of expressing by ballot our choice of rulers for this Government which our brothers so gallantly served; and ask that hereafter we may aid loyalty in suppressing any future attempts at its overthrow.

We make this demand as one of right, if not of expediency, and are unwilling to believe that a powerful, rating people, strengthened by new victories with the aid of our hands, could be less magnanimous in purpose and in action, less consistent with the true theory of a sound democracy, than to concede to us our claims. We believe that with expediency even our demands are not at war, but that with right does public policy strike hands and invite our votes, as it did our muskets, to the maintenance of authority over the disorganizing elements which attend a returning peace.

We have too much faith in the permanency of this Government to believe that the extension of the elective franchise to a few loyal black men could unsettle its foundations or violate a single declaration of its rights.

If our demands were not clothed with justice, we, whose very flesh still wears the scars of slavery, could hardly claim for ourselves that privilege which, enjoyed in the past by our late masters, enabled them to make cringing subjects of us all.

But we are no longer cowed beneath the name of chattels and of brutes, but we own ourselves, our families, and our homes; and as men demand that this freedom shall bear the spirit as well as the form—that we shall not be mocked with palsied hands and made helpless in our own defense—that the skeleton of liberty may be clothed with flesh and blood in order that we ourselves may resist the tyranny of the "unfriendly legislation" of our late masters and their sympathizers, who for four years past have been fighting to enslave our bodies and souls.

Among those who just now manifest so much solicitude and sympathy in our behalf, and who are so anxious to do for us our voting, to perform all our legislation, and to accept all our political responsibilities, do we chiefly discover the very men whose votes once made us slaves and chattels, and robbed the chastity of our homes, when we had no friend to counsel or law to protect us from their vandal hands and black hell-born codes.

If we are to be nursed and strengthened into manhood solely at the hands of others, we ask, in the name of God, that it be done by our friends and not by our enemies.

But we seek not to impose our tutelage or our cares upon others; we ask the privilege of being no longer a burden on the body politic, and that no longer we be made the subject of endless discussion and legislation, but are willing to carry these responsibilities ourselves in common with every other citizen.

With President Johnson do we claim that "loyal men, whether white or black, shall control our destinies." We ask that the "two streams of loyal blood which it took to conquer one, mad with treason," shall not be separated at the ballot-box—that he who can be trusted with an army musket, which makes victory and protects the Nation, shall also be intrusted with the right to express a preference for his rulers and his laws.

We are told that we are weak; hence we ask for those rights which make free men strong, and are ever deemed essential to the white man's confidence and courage.

We are told that we are ignorant; hence we ask for those lessons of experience in governing ourselves which, also, are ever deemed essential to the white man's advancement.

We are told that we are poor; hence we ask that by our own votes we may encourage our own industry, may make corporations for our capital, may charter our enterprises and give laws to our commerce, and, with the white man, be permitted to illustrate the axiomatic truth "that no man is so reliable as he who is intrusted with the welfare of his country," and is ever "more responsible when he goes to the ballot-box," as declared by Andrew Johnson.

We ask for a citizenship based upon a principle so broad and solid that upon it black men, white men, and every American born can equally, safely, and eternally stand.

John Mercer Langston, "Equality Before the Law," speech to the Hall of Representatives, Columbia, Missouri, January 9, 1866.

For Further Research

Herbert Aptheker, *Abolitionism: A Revolutionary Movement.* Boston: G.K. Hall/Twayne, 1989.

——, *American Negro Slave Revolts.* New York: International, 1965.

Henrietta Buckmaster, *Flight to Freedom: The Story of the Underground Railroad.* New York: Dell, 1972.

William Cheek and Aimee Lee Cheek, *John Mercer Langston and the Fight for Black Freedom, 1829–65.* Urbana: University of Illinois Press, 1989.

David Brion Davis, *The Problem of Slavery in Western Culture.* New York: Oxford University Press, 1988.

Carl Degler, *The Other South.* New York: Harper and Row, 1974.

David Herbert Donald, *Charles Sumner and the Coming of the Civil War.* Chicago: University of Chicago Press, 1960.

Martin Duberman, ed., *The Antislavery Vanguard.* Princeton, NJ: Princeton University Press, 1965.

Dwight Lowell Dumond, *Antislavery: The Crusade for Freedom in America.* Ann Arbor: University of Michigan Press, 1961.

Stanley Elkins, *Slavery: A Problem in American Institutional Life.* Chicago: University of Chicago Press, 1976.

Ena L. Farley, *The Underside of Reconstruction New York: The*

Struggle over the Issue of Black Equality. New York: Garland, 1993.

Donald E. Fehrenbach, *Prelude to Greatness.* Palo Alto, CA: Stanford University Press, 1962.

Louis Filler, *The Crusade Against Slavery, 1830–1860.* New York: Harper & Brothers, 1960.

Eric Foner, *Free Soil, Free Labor, Free Men.* New York: Oxford University Press, 1970.

Phillip S. Foner, *Frederick Douglass.* New York: Citadel, 1964.

Elizabeth Fox-Genovese, *Within the Plantation: Black and White Women of the Old South.* Chapel Hill: University of North Carolina Press, 1988.

John Hope Franklin, *From Slavery to Freedom.* New York: Alfred A. Knopf, 1979.

——, *Reconstruction: After the Civil War.* Chicago: University of Chicago Press, 1961.

V.P. Franklin, *Black Self-Determination: A Cultural History of African-American Resistance.* Brooklyn, NY: Lawrence Hill Books, 1992.

George M. Fredrickson, *The Arrogance of Race: Historical Perspectives on Slavery, Racism, and Social Inequality.* Middletown, CT: Wesleyan University Press, 1988.

William Freehling, *Road to Disunion.* New York: Oxford University Press, 1990.

Henry Louis Gates, ed., *The Classic Slave Narratives.* New York: Mentor, 1987.

Eugene Genovese, *The World the Slaveholders Made: Two Essays in Interpretation.* New York: Pantheon Books, 1969.

Stanley Harrold, *The Abolitionists and the South, 1831–1861.* Lexington: University Press of Kentucky, 1995.

Michael Holt, *The Political Crisis of the 1850s.* New York: Wiley, 1978.

James Oliver Horton, *Free People of Color: Inside the African American Community*. Washington, DC: Smithsonian Institution, 1993.

Charles Johnson, Patricia Smith, and WGBH, eds., *Africans in America: America's Journey Through Slavery*. San Diego: Harcourt Brace/Harvest, 1998.

Winthrop D. Jordan, *White over Black: American Attitudes Toward the Negro, 1550–1812*. Chapel Hill: University of North Carolina Press, 1968.

Aileen Kraditor, *Means and Ends in American Abolitionism*. New York: Ivan Dee, 1989.

Dan Lacy, *The Abolitionists*. New York: McGraw-Hill, 1978.

Gerda Lerner, *The Grimke Sisters from South Carolina*. New York: Schocken, 1967.

Stephen R. Lilley, *Fighters Against American Slavery*. San Diego: Lucent Books, 1998.

Leon Litwack, *Been in the Storm So Long*. New York: Random House, 1980.

Carleton Mabee, *Black Freedom: The Nonviolent Abolitionists from 1830 Through the Civil War*. London: Macmillan, 1970.

Waldo E. Martin Jr., *The Mind of Frederick Douglass*. Chapel Hill: University of North Carolina Press, 1984.

Henry Mayer, *All on Fire: William Lloyd Garrison and the Abolition of Slavery*. New York: St. Martin's, 1998.

Daniel J. McInerney, *The Fortunate Heirs of Freedom: Abolition and Republican Thought*. Lincoln: University of Nebraska Press, 1994.

James M. McPherson, *The Struggle for Equality: Abolitionists and the Negro in the Civil War and Reconstruction*. Princeton, NJ: Princeton University Press, 1964.

August Meier and Elliott Rudwick, *From Plantation to Ghetto*. New York: Hill & Wang, 1976.

James Miller, ed., *The Complete History of American Slavery*. San Diego: Greenhaven, 2001.

Edmund Morgan, *American Slavery, American Freedom*. New York: Norton, 1975.

Walter Dean Myers, *Now Is Your Time! The African-American Struggle for Freedom*. New York: HarperCollins, 1991.

Richard Newman and Marcia Sawyer, *Everybody Say Freedom: Everything You Need to Know About African-American History*. New York: Plume/Penguin, 1996.

Russell Nye, *Fettered Freedom: Civil Liberties and the Slave Controversy, 1830–1860*. East Lansing: Michigan State University Press, 1964.

James Oakes, *The Ruling Race: A History of American Slaveholders*. New York: Knopf, 1982.

———, *Slavery and Freedom: An Interpretation of the Old South*. New York: Knopf, 1990.

Stephen B. Oates, *With Malice Toward None: A Life of Abraham Lincoln*. New York: New American Library, 1981.

Nell Irvin Painter, *Sojourner Truth: A Life, a Symbol*. New York: W.W. Norton, 1996.

William S. Parsons and Margaret A. Drew, *The African Meeting House in Boston: A Sourcebook*. Boston: Museum of Afro-American History, 1992.

Jane Pease and William Pease, *They Who Would Be Free: Blacks' Search for Freedom, 1830–1861*. New York: Atheneum, 1974.

David M. Potter, *The Impending Crisis, 1848–1861*. New York: Harper & Row, 1976.

Benjamin Quarles, *Black Abolitionists*. New York: Oxford University Press, 1969.

C. Peter Ripley, ed., *Witness for Freedom: African American Voices on Race, Slavery, and Emancipation*. Chapel Hill: University of North Carolina Press, 1993.

Willie Lee Rose, *Slavery and Freedom*. New York: Oxford University Press, 1982.

Columbus Salley, *The Black One Hundred: A Ranking of the Most Influential African-Americans Past and Present*. New York: Citadel, 1994.

Shirley Samuels, ed., *The Culture of Sentiment: Race, Gender, and Sentimentality in Nineteenth-Century America*. New York: Oxford University Press, 1992.

Richard Sewell, *Ballots for Freedom: Anti-Slavery Politics, 1837–1861*. New York: Oxford University Press, 1976.

Kenneth M. Stamp, *The Peculiar Institution: Slavery in the Ante-Bellum South*. New York: Vintage Books, 1956.

James B. Stewart, *Holy Warriors*. New York: Hill & Wang, 1976.

Sterling Stuckey, *Slave Culture*. New York: Oxford University Press, 1987.

Larry Tise, *Proslavery: A History of the Defense of Slavery in America, 1701–1840*. Athens: University of Georgia Press, 1987.

Wendy Hamand Venet, *Neither Ballots nor Bullets: Women Abolitionists and the Civil War*. Charlottesville: University Press of Virginia, 1991.

C. Vann Woodward, *American Counterpoint*. Boston: Little, Brown, 1971.

Jean Fagan Yellin and John C. Van Horne, eds., *The Abolitionist Sisterhood: Women's Political Culture in Antebellum America*. Ithaca, NY: Cornell University Press, 1994.

Document Collections and Other Primary Sources

American Memory: Historical Collections for the National Digital Library, Library of Congress, Washington, D.C. http://memory.loc.gov.

The American Passages: A History of the United States. New York: Harcourt College, 1999.

Roy P. Basler, ed., *The Collected Works of Abraham Lincoln.* New Brunswick, NJ: Rutgers University Press, 1955. The Abraham Lincoln Association, 1953.

Ray Allen Billington, ed., *A Free Negro in the Slave Era: The Journal of Charlotte L. Forten.* New York: Collier Books, 1961.

Charles L. Blockson, *The Underground Railroad: Dramatic First-Hand Accounts of Daring Escapes to Freedom.* New York: Berkley Books, 1987.

Documenting the American South, an electronic archive of southern history, literature, and culture. Chapel Hill: University of North Carolina Press. http://metalab.unc.edu.

Douglass Archives of American Public Address (electronic archive). Evanston, IL: Northwestern University Press, 2000. http://pubweb.northwestern.edu.

Frederick Douglass, *Selected Speeches and Writings.* Ed. Philip S. Foner. New York: Da Capo, 1992.

Electronic Oberlin Group: Oberlin Through History, Oberlin College Archives. www.oberlin.edu.

Suzanne Pullon Fitch and Roseann M. Mandziuk, *Sojourner Truth as Orator Wit, Story, and Song.* Westport, CT: Greenwood, 1997.

From Slavery to Freedom: The African American Pamphlet Collection, Library of Congress, Rare Book and Special Collections, Washington, D.C.

Furman University, Nineteenth-Century Documents Project. www.furman.edu.

Deirdre Mullane, ed., *Crossing the Danger Water: Three Hundred Years of African-American Writing.* New York: Anchor Books/Bantam Doubleday/Dell, 1993.

Richard Newman, Patrick Rael, and Philip Lapsanksy, eds., *Pamphlets of Protest: An Anthology of Early African American Protest Literature, 1790–1860.* New York: Routledge, 2001.

C. Peter Ripley et al., eds., *The Black Abolitionist Papers.* Vol. 1. *The British Isles, 1830–1865.* Chapel Hill: University of North Carolina Press, 1985.

Yuval Taylor, ed., *I Was Born a Slave: An Anthology of Classic Slave Narratives* Chicago: Lawrence Hill Books, 1999.

Index